Thanks so much for Jeshua, The Personal Christ. *I love it. It reads like comfortable sunlight. I need but read a paragraph at a time, and it lasts as a kind of "light impression" on my thoughts for days.*

—Steve Haag
   San Jose, California

I was delighted with Jeshua, The Personal Christ, *and find it to be a wonderful comfort.*

—Holly Michaels
   Mt. Shasta, California

I am thanking you for Jeshua, The Personal Christ. *I have read it, I have enjoyed it, I have learnt from it, and I keep affirming, "I am an awakened Child of God." I find this very satisfying as it is encouraging us to open our mind to who we really are.*

—The Rev. W. E. Goodison-Orr
   Miami, Florida

I really love your Jeshua book. I think it's my favorite book.

—William Weeks
   Santa Fe, New Mexico

Thank you once again for a truly enlightening book. My dear friend Jeshua never disappoints. His gentle guidance illuminates my path, helps me dodge the potholes, and awakens me again to the creativity of my adventure. My heart is full of joy and peace.

—Adrienne Campbell
　Indian Head Park, Illinois

Jeshua
The Personal Christ

Messages from
Jeshua ben Joseph (Jesus)

Volume II

ISBN 1-878555-09-X

Second edition

Published by
Oakbridge University Press
www.Oakbridge.org
Judith@Oakbridge.org

*Heartfelt thanks to all, seen and unseen,
who have assisted in the preparation
of this book.*

Contents

The chapters in this book are based on transcripts of Jeshua messages given on Sunday mornings at the Oakbridge University Chapel or evening gatherings sponsored by the University.

Foreword

We are living at a time of rapid change and great transformation on the planet. Many of our old social structures and institutions are falling by the wayside; such upheaval forces us to look for deeper answers than the ones that once satisfied us. Everywhere we look, life is moving us to be bigger than we were or thought we could be.

At such a time we need to tap into the highest guidance available. No longer can we look to human thinking for our answers. Somehow, some way, we must rediscover the divine and open our minds and hearts to receive gifts beyond the ones we can manufacture through human thought.

The Jeshua material is a welcome and comforting gift to humanity poised on the brink of transformation. The voice of Jeshua is warm, insightful, and compassionate. He reminds us of our power and potential to manifest the divine destiny we have chosen. He reminds us that we can be who we are; in fact we must be who we are.

The message is simple, yet we must keep hearing it until we live it: Simply love. Love your divinity and love your humanity. Do not judge against yourself, for the spirit of God lives in you, as you. Do not seek outside yourself for the light, for the light is what you are.

As I read these pages my heart feels relaxed, safe, and at peace. I remember that we are all connected through an invisible bond of brotherhood and sisterhood. I rejoice in the fact that Spirit speaks to us in a language we can understand. God is willing to talk to us as we are, where we are.

I suggest you savor this book and really be with it. Rather than running through it intellectually, read a few sentences, put the book down for a moment and be with the message. Drink in the essence of these words like a fine wine. Let your soul be nourished. Read not just for information — indeed you have plenty of that — but read for inspiration. Become one with the material, so you know it belongs to you, for it does.

Jeshua reminds you, remember your holiness, for you lack nothing. Let this sacred text remind you that everything God is, you are; everything love fulfills, you deserve; every divine dream you wish to fulfill, you may manifest. Use this text as a steppingstone to the remembrance of your own divinity, and you will recognize that the love you seek is available to you right now.

Remember always the Truth...that you are Loved...Special...and Important!

— *Alan Cohen*

Beloved one,

I encourage you to remember
the time before time
when you played in the meadow
of your Father's Kingdom,
secure in His Love.

Claim now your birthright
as His only begotten Child,
the Christ,
and ascend unto Me.

Try On A New Sandal

Beloved one, it is my unbounded pleasure to remind you once again of the joy that you are. You are the Life of our Heavenly Father expressing upon this plane. You are the Child, the holy Child, the only Child of our Heavenly Father, and you are joy incarnate. Not always do you feel it. Not always do you express it, but always you are the holy Child whose birthright it is to play in the Kingdom. That is all that is asked of you: to be the Love which you are and to express it freely upon this plane; to choose in each moment which voice you will listen unto: whether it would be the voice of the world, of worry, of confusion, of doubt, of sorrow, *or* whether it would be to live in the joy which you are; to release the burdens of imagined guilt, called mistakes, and to release the necessity for material possessions, all of the trappings which mankind loves to carry about — now to say, "I am the joy of my Father wherever I find myself, with or without the material trappings. I am always — foremost and always — my Father's Child and I will go this day in the joy that I am. Tomorrow if I want to, I will pick up the worries again, but for this day, I will choose to abide in the house of my Father."

Now, I will share with you that the house of our Heavenly Father is one which is filled with great joy and singing, laughter, freedom and light, beauty — beauty in all forms — a house which is full of the creative joy that knows Itself to be unlimited, knows Itself to be one with every life form, and appreciates beauty in all life expression.

You are free in every moment to choose to *consciously* dwell in the house of your Father. If there have been aspects of your life which have not been of beauty, of joy, of health, happiness, love, you are free to close that chapter and to begin anew. Whatever quality in your life you would want to see magnified, developed, augmented, increased, dwell upon that quality. Know that you have choice regarding where you will abide and what you will shine the light of your countenance upon. If it be the quality of understanding, relating to the brothers and sisters and what they are going through, how they are seeing things; if it be the quality of tolerance, of allowance, of seeing the Christ in everyone who stands before you;

dwell upon the quality of love, and ask it to share with you its fullness. Ask it to share with you its companionship in every moment.

If it be the quality of courage, abide in the heart with that quality and ask, "How does it feel to be the courage of Who I know myself to be — the holy Child of the Heavenly Father, totally unlimited Love expressing upon this plane?" And then you will look at whatever situation is in front of you, whatever relationship, and you will see yourself as the power of Love, totally unbounded by what the world would speak unto you, and you will know that your courage comes from the Truth of your being.

If you would know joy in your life, abide in the heart with the quality and the expression of joy. How does it feel to be the holy Child of the Heavenly Father, totally and unconditionally loved and accepted? How does it feel to be spontaneous, to speak from the heart the Truth of the Father, and to speak it fearlessly for there is nothing in the world to fear? You are the holy Child of our Heavenly Father, created before time began, perfect, upon whom there is no judgment.

All of the experiences you have had, all of the journeys you have been upon, have been as a great adventure for the very purpose of experiencing the infinite creativity of the holy Child which you are. You have been every life that you can imagine. You have expressed as every form that you can imagine, for as you call to mind different lifetimes, different expressions, know that you have lived those expressions. And as you relate to the one known as Christ, know you that you are the Christ.

Whatever quality you would see manifest in your experience, ask it to manifest *with* you and *as* you in every choice you make. Ask it to be your constant companion in each new day. Shine the light of your countenance upon whatever you would see magnified in your life.

For truly, as you shine your Light upon it, guess what happens? It grows. As you are willing to shine the light of your countenance — your consciousness, your awareness, your attention — upon the quality, the aspect, you would see magnified in your life, you will find it popping up everywhere.

You will find friends coming unto you, smiling and sharing the love with you, for they will feel the Love that you are willing to claim and they will want to be in your presence. If you would see harmony in your life and in your affairs, know that you are already that harmony. You are the Love and the order of our Heavenly Father and there is nothing that happens by chance — even though there are times that you would like to put responsibility outside of yourself and say, "I did not cause that. I would not ask for that. That could not be." And yet, in that moment it is your judgment to see it in denial; however, everything that happens is as a gift for you. It is as a messenger for you. It is nothing more — and nothing less — than a messenger. It is neutral.

It is your judgment how you will look upon it. And, as you have seen, because of the shifts in perception which you have been willing to make in what you would see as this journey already, the reactions that have been made out of habit last a smaller time interval before the awareness comes up that, "I can choose anew. I do not need to abide with the voice of the world. I do not need to continue in sorrow, in confusion. I am my Heavenly Father's only Child and I lack for nothing" — including the answer to whatever has been troubling you.

And if there seems to be something missing in your life at this moment, know that there is a message there for you. Take it deeply within the consciousness and ask yourself, "What is the message, the deeper message? Perhaps it is not missing at all, but it is there in a different form. How can I see this anew?" For there are many levels of messages which you present unto yourself — many levels — and you will discern one meaning upon the surface, and as you have the willingness to look and to sit with the messenger, with the circumstance, with the person, there will be other levels revealed unto you. Then you will come away from the experience with a treasure chest of insights — the in-sights from the inner knowing — and you will come to know that no one and no circumstance has power over you.

There is great strength coming from every experience. Many times you manifest occurrences in your life and you judge yourself quickly to be failing, to be lacking, to have not done well enough. And you say, "This would not have occurred if I had done such and such or if I had known such and such," and you stop at that point, not knowing that it is as the coin which has two sides. For as you would be looking upon the supposed weakness, what it is truly showing you is your strength. It is showing you your creativity. It is showing you the depth of your soul. It is showing you the infinite wisdom which you are in the heart. It is showing you the courage that you pull forth from what you would feel as the depths of your being to face every experience.

It is not to show you your weakness. It is to show you your strength. It is to show you the very qualities which you would, perhaps, feel to be beyond you: "Perhaps someone else has those qualities, but I sure don't." Have you ever said that?

Stop and look further. Stop and choose anew. For the very messenger that you would interpret as showing you your weaknesses is showing you your strengths. It is showing you your creativity, your wisdom, your very flexibility to deal with different situations as they come up and to choose anew to see them in a new perception.

You are the joy of the holy Child. Change any program that would speak to you of heaviness. Change it to lightness. Be willing to look on the other side of the coin. Be willing to ask, even as you sit in a place of confusion and sorrow and doubt and you feel yourself to be surrounded by a black cloud that seems impenetrable, be willing to sit with that black cloud and to ask of it, "What do you have to share with me?" And if it rains on you, so what? You will be cleansed!... I jest with you, and yet, as you are willing to abide in peace with the issue, you will see the black cloud dissolving as a mist. And in its place there will come a faint glimmer of light which will grow to reveal the next step — perhaps not the whole pathway but the next step — and that is all you need to know in any moment.

Be willing to consider a new perception; be ready and willing in every moment to ask, "How can I see this another way? How would it feel to take on the shoes of a new perception?"

"How would it feel to take on the shoes of someone else and walk in their sandals? Would it give me a different perception of how it feels for them to go about in this world?"

Be willing to try on the new sandal, the new perception, and to walk a mile or two in someone else's sandals. *And*, be willing to try on the new sandal, the new perception, about yourself and how *you* walk this world.

I would share with you what you would call a tool for trying on the new sandal, a tool for coming Home again.

Take a moment now to abide in the heart of silence and to take a deep breath. Breathe in the golden white Light that you are. Breathe it deeply into the very cells of the body.

Breathe in the golden white Light and exhale the Love that you are.

Breathe in the golden white Light and feel it expanding the Light of every cell in the body. Feel yourself to be Light.

And abiding in the place of Lightness, the peaceful place of the Heart, call unto yourself your very name. Think of your name and call yourself. Speak your name very lovingly — for truly you are Love — and speak unto yourself your own name as your Heavenly Father calls you.

Call unto yourself your name. Take your name deeply within your heart and call yourself, gently, softly. Speak unto yourself as your Heavenly Father speaks to you, for truly He calls unto you in every moment. Call your name as your Heavenly Father calls you. Feel the love that is in your name. Feel the love that your Heavenly Father showers upon you. Say your name to yourself in love, for your Father loves you with an everlasting Love.

Rest in the heart with your name, for truly you have chosen your name for the very qualities that it expresses. It is not by accident.

Call yourself with the Love of the Heavenly Father. Say your name with gentleness. Whisper it with love. Feel yourself enveloped in a cloud of acceptance which has never seen you other than perfect. Abide in the feeling of acceptance, total acceptance. Rest in the love. Know that peace to be your very nature.

This is the place of the Heart. This is the place of stillness, of sacred peace, of all wisdom. It is the place of Love.

Breathe in the golden white Light. See it lighting every cell of the body.

Whenever the world would come crushing in about you with its doubts and confusions, its sorrow, its activities, pause and return again unto the place of the Heart, the place where you know Love.

You can return unto this place at any time for you know it well. You know it now. Take this feeling with you as a touchstone for whenever things would be too hurried, too active. Pause, breathe and remember Love.

Walk often in the sandals of Love —love of self and others. Walk lightly, unconstricted by the attitudes and habitual judgments of the world. Try on the new sandal of Love. It comes in your size.

Play in the Sandbox

Holy Child, do you know who you are?

You are the Christ. You are a great ray of Light, ever ongoing and ever expressing. You have chosen to put the focus of your attention upon this time and this space, this personality and this body, and you do it very well for you have practiced, in what you would see as many lifetimes, being the personality, being the body, and yet, you are much more than the body and the personality with which you identify.

You are a great ray of Light. The energy which you are is what attracts the molecules of physicality unto you to form the body that expresses, that walks about, that laughs, that cries, that hugs.

You are a great ray of Light. Take that deeply within the consciousness. Abide in the heart with what that means. You are a great ray of Light. Totally unlimited, totally unbounded by what the world would say unto you. Totally unbounded by what you would say unto yourself. In moments of confusion, moments of doubt, stop and pause. Return again unto the place of silence and ask what your Heavenly Father would say unto you. Walk in the sandals of the Heavenly Father and view your brothers and sisters *and yourself* as your Heavenly Father sees you: His only creation, Light divine, experienced as Love.

You are the holy Child of our Heavenly Father. You are as I am. You are as all of the qualities which have been ascribed unto the Christ, for you are Christ. You are my brother. You are my sister. You have chosen to express upon this plane with what you would see as the physicality, and yet you are much more than the body and the circumstances that you surround yourself with.

You are totally unlimited. Whatever the heart would speak unto you, whatever the heart desires, is within your power to manifest, for truly you are manifesting every moment what you see in your world — and if what you see does not speak to you of love and of expansiveness, know that you can change what you see.

Nothing Real can be threatened. It cannot be threatened because Reality has been before time began, before the holy Child thought to bring forth all Adventures, all worlds. And you have gone nowhere from the Kingdom. The Kingdom of your Reality is within you, *as you*, and you can never be apart from it or from the Father.

That is my message of good news. That is my gospel. You have heard me say, "I and the Father are one," and you, because you are not separate from me, because you are also the holy and only Child of our Heavenly Father, you and the Father are one, and you abide in His Kingdom forever. There you abide in omnipresent joy and total peace and all power — not as the world would define power, but the power of the Truth of your being, of Who you are.

You need accept no one's image of you — or even your image of yourself. Accept only the image of the Child which you are, the holy Child. Know that you are the peace of the Kingdom. Know that you can carry that peace into every situation. And as you do so, ones will come unto you and, being in your presence, they will feel a healing presence. Abiding in the peace that you are, you offer unto your brothers and sisters the opportunity to connect with the peace that they are, the healing peace which cannot be threatened, for it is your Reality.

Therefore, as you would look upon troubling situations, know that yes, in one sense these events have a reality. Yes, there may be a feeling of loss and of sorrow, but there is also presented the opportunity to look beyond and to know holy vision, to see events within the context of the Whole. There may be presented the opportunity to know that the laying down of the body does not mean the cessation of life, for Life is truly ever ongoing and eternal. And even those who would be caught very much in the confusion and chaos and the sorrow of feeling a lack will come unto a place of knowing the presence of Love and will know that their loved one has not gone from them. They will have opportunity to remember that this has been experienced in all of what they would see as lifetimes, and that as one body is laid down, just as easily and as quickly another is raised up.

Those who you would see as having laid down the body and having made the choice to go on to a new experience, many are already choosing to collect unto themselves the molecules of physicality again and to express with form again.

Life is an ever-ongoing expression, and it matters not whether you are expressing with what you would see as the molecules of this physicality in this design pattern or if you are expressing as what you would know as the Light beings — for truly, you are a Light being — or expressing as what you would see as using the molecules of another kind of physicality in another realm, another universe, another planet — a different formation, a different design pattern, perhaps a more fluid physicality, but Life nonetheless.

And if you will receive it, as you relate unto the concept of expressing Life in other forms — perhaps a more fluid form or one with more density — know you that you have expressed and are expressing in life forms differing from what you have chosen to express with in this point of focus. For truly, this is but a point of focus. You are also, even at what you would see as this time, expressing in other galaxies, other dimensions, other realms. You are truly unlimited. So the next time someone would come unto you and give you what you might call a hard time, or give you what would be seen as a challenge, you can say unto that one, "That may be your truth, but my Truth is that I am unlimited, and even right now I am expressing as my Heavenly Father's Child in other dimensions and other galaxies, if you will." It will give them pause for thought.

It might even change what you would see as the outcome of that situation, for they will have to ponder, "Could there be more than just what I see in front of me? More than what I experience just with the five senses? Maybe there *is* more." And, if you will receive it, you *are* more.

Know also that as you express upon other planes, in other dimensions, you are expressing in what would be seen as other time frames. You are truly unlimited. You are the Child of the Heavenly Father and you are playing.

You have many sandboxes in which you play. You express in many dimensions, many realms, many sandboxes. It is not just that you express in the sandbox of this focus of attention.

It is not just that you express in the sandbox of where you would feel your place of employment to be. That is one sandbox, and then you come unto the family that you live with and share relationship with, and that is another sandbox of experience. And sometimes you will pack up some of the belongings and you will travel unto another place, and you will be in interchange of expression with your brothers and sisters in another sandbox.

And sometimes as you sit in meditation and you allow yourself to expand to knowing your holiness, you go unto another sandbox, the sandbox of eternity, and you know yourself to be the Child playing in eternity. You know yourself to be the great ray of Light which plays in all of the sandboxes.

Nothing Real can be threatened. You, as the holy Child that you are, cannot be threatened. You cannot be threatened by the voice of the world, by the voice of your brothers and sisters who would speak unto you their image of you. You cannot be threatened by the fears that would come up. You cannot be threatened by the image of yourself that you hold.

What is Real cannot be threatened. What is unreal — fear, limited self-image or limited image of who your brothers and sisters are, and the perceptions predicated on these limitations — does not exist. Therein lies the peace of God, and your joy.

Go with great joy in your heart. Know that, as the holy Child which you are, nothing can threaten you. Nothing can harm you. It never has and it never will. Play in the sandbox, know it to be a sandbox, and enjoy.

On Meditation

Beloved one, I would speak with you now about meditation. There is not a day that goes by that you do not spend some time in meditation, for there are various levels of what you would call meditation.

If it be only as you pause in the first moments of your morning to behold the beauty of the light which comes with each dawn, and you allow yourself to relax and to breathe in deeply the breath of the holy living Spirit which you are, that is an instant of meditation.

It does not have to be what you would see as a ritual, of sitting in a certain posture, of sitting for a certain length of time, of lighting a candle or of having incense. All of these are beautiful additions to meditation and they can be beneficial ways of bringing one's focus to the connection of the Spirit that you are, but they are not meditation. Meditation is returning again unto the place of the Heart, to the deep peace of your Being.

To bring yourself to the quiet place of the Heart, allow the breath to slow, to deepen. The simplicity of one deep breath restores to you the opportunity to abide in the center of your Being. Focusing on the breath, watching the breath, *allowing* the breath with ease, you may abide in meditation. With practice, you may extend the time spent in meditation, until you find yourself abiding in peace amidst the activity of your day.

In each moment of your timing practice the presence of knowing the peace that passes the understanding of the world. In every activity that you would do, pause for a moment and ask, "Who is doing this activity? Who is breathing? Who is moving? Who is touching?" Be very present with whatever you are doing and know that that Presence is the Life of your Father upon this plane.

When you behold another and you smile at them in greeting, pause and ask yourself, "Who is smiling?" and know that it is your Heavenly Father expressing upon this plane as you. Each word of support, of respect, of honor is the word of Love of the Heavenly Father. Each step that you take is a step that He takes. In each moment practice the Presence of the holy Spirit, the spirit of Wholeness. Practice the Presence of Love, of Who and What you are.

Another avenue of meditation which proceeds from the awareness of the Presence is the process of contemplative meditation, in which process you take an idea, a concept, and abide in communion with the idea or concept, taking it back to its very root source, for there are levels upon levels upon levels of meaning, each one revealing more and more of the Truth of your Being.

Moreover, you may behold an object, and as you look upon that object, think of the process which has brought it to your hand. Feel yourself to be one with the object that is in front of you. Know that its very energy is you — expressing in another form — but it is you. It would not exist without your consciousness. Feel yourself to be one, to meld as the energy that you know yourself to be and to fuse with the energy of the object. Know that there is no separation.

And as you have come to experience oneness with an object, know that there is no separation between you and what you would see as another body, one of your brothers and sisters. All hearts are joined. It is only when you look with the eyes of the body and you see what would be separate bodies, packages, that you think that there is separation, but the energy which you are knows no boundaries.

The Love which I am is the Love that you are. The smile you extend is the Love that we are. The innocence of the eye is the innocence of the holy Child of the Heavenly Father, and there is no separation.

If you will receive it, I would suggest that you sit with a flower in the morning of your timing. Spend a whole day watching the flower unfold. Watch as it opens each tiny petal as the energy which it is, as Life expressing. Allow your consciousness to feel at one with its expression. And as you sit and contemplate the flower unfolding, you will come to know an intimacy which has its roots in oneness. The very process that allows the flower to express is your process as well: the process of simple beauty, of simple Life unfolding.

Practice the Presence of Life in each moment. Take the Father consciously into every activity. You express the Creative Energy in each moment whether you are aware of it or not — and it is much more enlivening and enlightening to be aware of what you are doing.

The ultimate level of meditation is one which comes from the process of practicing the Presence of Who you are, through the process of contemplative meditation, to the realization of the Oneness with everything and everyone that you behold. For through that process you return again unto the place of Peace, the sacred energy of Oneness which transforms all worlds.

This has been called nirvana. It has been called bliss. It is called atonement, at-one-ment, where you know yourself to be not the separate self with the small "s," but you know your Self with a capital "S."

You know your Self to meld with the pool of Love, knowing that you are all power — not as the world would define power, but all power because of your beingness — all creativity, all Love, from before time began. And when the purpose of time has been fulfilled, you will remain, as you have always been, the One holy Child, unlimited.

You are not limited by anything that you would think, by any concept, by any belief, by any philosophy, by any teaching that anyone would give unto you. You are not limited by any image you have held of yourself or by any image anyone else has held of you. Nothing you have ever done or said or thought has ever changed Who you are. Nothing anyone else has ever done or said — to you or about you — or thought has ever changed Who you are.

Now you are beginning to remember Who you are. I come to share with you what would be like sparkplugs — ideas which will give you a glimpse of Who you are — but I cannot unfold it in its fullness for you. Only you can tap the pool of Love that you are. Only you can become alive with the fire of Who you are. Only you can know the dynamic quality of Love that is your true nature, holy Child in and through and beyond all universes.

Only you can know the joy of unconditional acceptance of self and others as you claim the Truth of your being.

You are a great ray of Light, totally unlimited, unbounded. You are the Love of the Heavenly Father expressing upon this plane in the design and in the fashion which you have chosen. And if there be moments of doubt, if there be moments of sadness, you can embrace and release them. First, acknowledge that you experience a particular emotion; embrace it as your experience. Then ask of it, using the process of contemplative meditation, what its gift is for you. Make a friend of that emotion. If it be the emotion of sorrow, do not fear the tears. Allow them to flow freely, for as they flow they will give unto you a vision, a lightening of the heart, a balancing.

If it be the emotion of anger, feel it in its fullness. Embrace it, own it, express it — but not to the detriment of a brother or sister who may be sharing space with you. Allow yourself to contemplate in dynamic quality what the anger is telling you. What is the root fear?

You can be as angry, as energetic, as sorrowful, as full of tears, as need be and you will abide, for your emotions will not devastate you. They will be well spent. Know you "spending" — when you go to the store and you spend? You give it in exchange. The emotions will be spent and they will give you in exchange a deeper message about yourSelf.

Everything you see occurring in your life is there as a gift for you. It is there as the messenger who would deliver unto you the Western Union telegram, and it comes with a message for you to read.

Take every occurrence, every interaction, every *re*-action into meditation, to contemplate, to receive fully the blessing of its message. Abide in the Heart of Wholeness as you behold self, and as you behold a sister, a brother. Then, that which has been seen as unholy will transform before your very eyes into holy understanding, in which there is now only the Love of our Father.

Meditation, beloved one, means entering into the secret place of the Most High, the heart of Love. As often as you remember, return to the place of peace within, and, abiding in silence, listen for the still, small Voice which speaks to you from before time began. You are your Father's holy Child, in whom He is well pleased. Commune with Him often in the gift of meditation.

You've Gone As Far As You Can Go

Beloved and holy Child of our Father, when first you thought to be upon what you now call our holy Mother, the Earth, you came as the Light being you are. You came with the creativity of the holy Child to see, "What more can I create?"

For, verily, before time began, you, as the Child of the Creator, flexed your figurative creative wings, and as one great Thought to experience the beauty of energy in form, you imagined, put the images into action, and brought forth energy into form.

Now, the Thought energy did not coalesce right away, for there would be — although this was just the beginning of what you have called time — eons of time before the form would come into what you now recognize and know. The Earth, the planets, the universes were/are very much a Light energy and you were/are Light energy, and the forms which you brought forth were nebulous, cloud-like. You knew yourself to be Light, and your creations were Light. You were very much one with what you *are* creating — for truly, it is not an event which has happened a long time ago; it is what is happening moment by moment as the Light and the Consciousness that you are.

And as the Earth came into being, you thought to create upon and out of the substance of Earth. You thought to bring together frequencies and vibrations of the Light into various combinations to see what would result. And with those thoughts were born the clouds, the energies of the oceans, of the rivers, of the streams, and the more dense material known as the mountains and the hills in their various formations.

In due time, you thought to experience life upon this plane, and you came as the Light being, not with the attraction of the molecules of physicality which you see yourself now surrounded by —and very beautiful they are — but you came as the Light being to experience, "What would it feel like to be upon what I have created?" And you went as the wind, flowing as the Light. And you went with your thought from mountaintop to sea level, beneath the sea to the mountains that are beneath the water, and you thought to experience how it would feel to be in expression with form.

You experimented creating different forms, collecting the molecules of physicality unto you, and you experienced life expression in many different forms: as the very mountains themselves, as the blade of grass, as the tiniest flower and as the largest tree.

And you collected the molecules of physicality to yourself in a form which could express in fluidity of motion, and you ran and you flew with ease. Think you now how it would feel to fly. Can you imagine how it would feel to fly from one tree branch to another, on to the top of the highest tree, and to see from that perspective the blade of grass upon the Earth?

Know you, that as you can imagine, you have experienced. For truly, you cannot imagine that which you have not experienced. It would not be within your knowing.

And as time — as you would see it in the process of the belief system — evolved, you became more and more immersed in the expression of physicality, to the degree that you no longer knew yourself to be the Light being, and life was seen to be one of survival upon this plane. Many lifetimes you have lost yourself in the identification with dense physical form.

You are now awakening from the place of limited identity, the place of density. You have gone as deeply into forgetfulness as you are going to go, and you are well on your way to remembering the Light being which you are, the totally unlimited Child of our Heavenly Father. For even in your most limited belief system there was still a small Voice, somewhere in the recesses of your mind, saying, "Perhaps there could be more than this. Perhaps there is more to Life." And you questioned what life is all about. The questioning has brought you now to the place where you are asking to experience your unlimitedness: "Who am I? Perhaps I am more than the body and the personality with which I identify. Perhaps I am more than the role I play in certain relationships. Perhaps I am more than the nine-to-five identity that earns the golden coins. There must be more." And as you are allowing yourself to experience expanded self-image, you are feeling yourself to be lighter. Thus dawns the Age of Enlightenment.

Yes, the Age of Enlightenment has to do with wisdom, as has been believed. It is inner wisdom, and the wisdom is predicated upon and flows from the awareness of the Light you are. Furthermore, beloved one, the enlightenment comes not only in the thoughts and emotions, but even in the body itself, allowing the very cells of the body to express the Light which they are.

There is now a wake-up call which is sounding with great clarity, a call which you are responding to. If you were not, you would not find yourself in conversation with me. If you are reading these words, know that your soul, your individuality, has called out to know Who you are, to experience the grandeur and holiness of that which you are.

It is my joy to be able to converse with you in this manner, to serve as Friend, as Brother, to hold you in my Love until you remember it as your own. I come to remind you that life need not be a heavy experience; you are lightness Itself. You are the Light that you bring to every experience, and now you are beginning to release your habitual identification with density.

You are beginning to remember the holy Child, created before time began. As you behold everyone and everything with the eyes of Christ — and if you define that to be my eyes, that is okay, but I would share with you, they are your eyes as well — you will come to know that everyone you behold is the holy Child of God upon their path, discovering — which is what all of this is about —their own creativity and expressing it according to how they see it at that moment. It may not be as you would desire to see it; and sometimes in your musing you would say, "I would not have chosen to do such and such," and perhaps you would not choose that now. But I share with you, you have, in times past. For you have experienced all.

There is an awakening occurring now upon the Earth, and you have heard the wake-up call to rise up out of density. It has been prophesied that in the Awakening there will be a grand upliftment, an ascension of the physical bodies. And this may happen, as you choose. However, if you will receive it, you have already ascended the body in what you would see as other lifetimes. For as you read these words and think about what is known as ascension, allowing the imagination free rein, how would it feel to ascend? Can you imagine how it would feel to have all of the molecules of the cells of the body filled with so much Light that you would be as a helium balloon and just arise, lighter than air, no longer taking yourself — and others — so heavily?

In the time of awakening upon this plane, there will be ascension. Many of you will choose to ascend the body, quite literally, by allowing it to be the Light it is, by infusing it with more of the Light energy which you are. But more important than the experience of physical ascension is the ascension in consciousness: allowing yourself to remember the Light you are, to feel yourself to be radiance, to know yourself to be unlimited, to be loved with an everlasting Love. As you have experienced moments of love which have uplifted you out of what has been the ordinary expression of everyday life, you have felt yourself transported to a place of ascension.

You have asked to remember, and what is desired in the heart will be made manifest.

As you are uplifted in consciousness, you will draw all men — and women — to that higher state of remembrance. "I, if I be lifted up, will draw all men unto me." This is truly what the Age of Enlightenment is all about. For each moment as you allow yourself to rise up in consciousness, you uplift all of creation.

In the coming days there may be — and will be — the physical ascension of the body. In the coming days there may be — and will be — the ascension of consciousness: the ascension where you allow the Spirit which you are to feel Its freedom, to feel Its joy, knowing yourself to be the unlimited holy Child of our Heavenly Father. Abide in joy.

The Descent Into Matter

Beloved one, you are the energy of Light and beyond. You are totally unlimited, always ongoing, expressing and experiencing as Love. You are Love incarnate, in and through the body, activating the body. You have chosen to express with the molecules of physicality upon this plane, attracting those molecules in the design pattern with which you now identify. In what you would see as other lifetimes you have expressed with other design patterns, *and* you have known other forms of expression within other dimensions.

You have activated other design patterns that you would find, in this lifetime, totally strange, and totally wonderful. For you have known expression, if you will receive it, as the angel, as the Light being which you are. You have known the fluidity of Light as the liquid drop of water — although it is not water — in the form of expression upon other planes. You have known expression as Thought, changing form from one moment to the next, as shape shifters. You have known dense expression of all variations, all sizes, all frequencies.

You are the ones who, as Light beings, chose to experience what it would be like to bring Spirit into matter. And having formed matter, you came as the Light being and you played upon the Holy Mother in a very fluid form, very much in awareness, conscious awareness, of the Light and the energy that you are. And then you thought to experience what it would be like to be with the form of matter, your creations, and to be awake, knowing yourself to be the activating Spirit and to experience the laws of matter. And this was done for what you would see as a long period of time.

In time, you became so mesmerized by your creations, so caught up in matter itself, that the focus of attention became identified with matter. Now, the focus of attention upon matter was not a mistake or a wrong-doing, for the creative holy Child desired to experience matter and to experience it fully.

The shift of focus from spirit to matter, from activating Isness to form, has been called a fall from grace, but it is not a fall as in what you would define

— and have, in your priestly lifetimes, identified — as sin. It is a descent into matter, yes. There has been a selection of frequency of vibration attuned to the physical in order to make it seemingly solid, or more dense. And with the descent into matter, accompanied by the conscious experience of matter, there has been a temporary fall from the *remembrance* of grace, the Love of the Father, the Spirit which activates the form.

And there are those of you who, in the very first experiments of being with physical form, ran into more solid structures and released the body. And there were those of you who had experiences with the other creations which you put upon the face of our holy Mother, the Earth, such as the animals, and discovered the body to be food for the animals. You then decided that perhaps there needed to be some modification of the experiment, and you became a bit swifter afoot and a bit more wise in ways of protecting the body.

Through all of this there came about a sense of identification with the body, so that the focus was more and more upon the physical expression and less and less upon the spiritual nature that you are. And as the identification shifted, there was less and less knowing of the spiritual nature, and more and more of a calling out of the physical, of the material, that would demand your attention and protection.

What if I were to tell you that all that has happened is in order? All of the process of Awakening is in order. All of the process of what has been known as the Descent is in order. It was not a mistake. It was not something for which you need feel guilty. It is not something where you have sinned and gone astray. The descent into matter to experience bringing Spirit into matter was very much planned and ordained. You planned it and you ordained that there would be the experience — and you also left your request with the Front Desk for the Wake-up call which is happening now.

Many of your lifetimes you have believed, and many of your religious organizations would speak unto you, that you have sinned and gone astray, that you are unworthy of the Father's Love because of an original sin which you don't even remember making. You have never sinned. You have never made mistakes. You have made *choices*. You have done what you have desired to experience — and this is true in every event in your life, every relationship in your life.

You are the holy Child who desired to experience matter and to bring yourself into the expression of matter as the body, as the chair upon which you sit, as the electricity which is you in extension. You desired to experience what it would be like to be Spirit incarnate in the body — and this is truly what you are being asked, now, to do: to become one hundred percent incarnate as the Spirit that you are.

Not to just bring the part of your awareness that the body would dictate, but to bring all of the total Self that you are into awareness and to express with the molecules of physicality in an awake state.

The laws of matter are ones which you brought into being, from the belief of relationship of part to whole — what you would call mathematical relationship — and you wished to experience these laws fully, to know exactly how it feels to be as matter. Not just to observe your creations, but to be in expression as that creation. This is why you can sit and imagine what it would feel like to be the beloved pet, how it would feel to be the eagle that soars so high above, how it feels to be the process of the flower that unfolds. As you sit in your quiet time of meditation, you can go within and experience what it feels like to be the mountain, the tree, the flowing water, the horse that runs so freely in the wind — and even the lowly slug.

You are Spirit expressing as matter. You are the holy Child of our Heavenly Father, and it is a grand expression that you do upon this plane. It is not a heavy responsibility, although your world would speak to you of heaviness, of the "have to's" and the "shoulds," and would judge you if you do not come up to whatever standard is in fashion at the moment. You are the holy Child desiring to be Spirit — which you are — incarnate — which you are — and desiring to be fully awake and aware in each moment.

There is an awakening upon this plane. It is as a wave which sweeps across the face of our Holy Mother, the Earth, an awakening to the Truth that all life-forms are of the creative Light energy, and that you are connected, not just interdependent, but as one. For truly, you are one as the Light, expressing as the creations you have brought forth. Even your very body is your creation, and when you are finished with it, it will return unto the holy Mother from whence it has come.

And when and if you desire to express with another body, you will call forth the molecules from the holy Mother, the Earth — or from another collection of energy known as a planet or plane of expression — using the power of the Heavenly Father which you are, and you will call them forth in a design pattern which will serve you in what you will see as that incarnation.

And does it mean that, "If I don't get it this lifetime, I will have to come back and experience it until I get it?" It does not. It is always a choice, as it is in every moment. For the laws of matter have no power over you, and the holy instant of Remembrance is not bound by time or place or lifetime.

You are the Spirit which is dictating what the laws of matter are, and in each moment you choose how you will interact with the laws of matter. That is why matter can be changed in an instant. That is why ones will experience instantaneous healing. For truly, in each moment you are reborn. In each moment you are the Thought which holds together the design pattern that expresses. *In each moment you are reborn.* Think upon what power — not as the world defines power — but what power you *are* that enables you to keep the design pattern together moment by moment to express. It is no small miracle.

The descent into matter has been by choice and by design. The ascension from limited identification is by choice and by design. And in each moment the choice is yours to ascend. Does this mean to go afar off somewhere unto the clouds, to look down upon your brothers and sisters who would still be sleeping? No, it does not. It means to be very much where you are, expressing with the body, and to be awake, to know that you are Spirit activating the body, to know that you are Spirit incarnate.

You will still go to your place of employment if you so desire. You will still be in interaction with your brothers and sisters, expressing the Love that you are. You will still be in service, but it will be with a new understanding. You will be coming, as they say, from a different space: the space of knowing Who you are. It is a grand journey we have been on. It has not been a mistake. Do not judge yourself for having fallen asleep, for having chosen to know form. It was part of what you chose to experience — and of what I chose to experience in my incarnations, even in the incarnation known as Jeshua ben Joseph. It has been with purposeful design, and now the next part of the design is at hand: the Awakening and the Ascension.

Arise up, holy Child of our Father.

Falling In Love
Ascending in Love

All of you have found yourselves, at some time, falling in love. All of you have fallen head over heels in love. And you have found yourself to be a new person. You have wondered, "Who is this person I feel myself to be? I am doing things now that I would only have imagined. I've seen others of my brothers and sisters act this way, but I didn't think I would. And yet I find myself most excited to think about this other person, to be with this other person, to share, finding that there is great excitement in coming together, asking, 'How was your day? What went on for you? What new insight? What happened?'" And you could not wait until you were in that one's presence again to share of the heart.

You feel yourself to be *alive* in that love. And that is so. That is why so many of your brothers and sisters fall in love over and over again. You have looked upon society, the brothers and sisters, in the recent years and you have wondered why there is so much of the changing of relationships. They try one relationship for awhile and then they say, "I want a new one. I want to start over."

It has always been thus, even in times when there was not perhaps the obvious change of partners, but it has been thus for much of your adventure. Ones have looked beyond the immediate relationship and have found themselves admiring the grass in another pasture and felt that the grass somewhere else was a bit greener — for a time — until they came unto the awakening and looked upon their own heart and found that love was right there all the time.

It is the way of mankind/womankind to want to experience falling in love, to have the feeling of being alive, the dynamic aliveness which makes every day feel worth living, an excitement. And underlying the search for human love is the desire to know the very dynamic Love which is your true nature.

You have found yourself, throughout many of what you would see as lifetimes, in relationship — some of them happy, some of them challenging. And you have "taught" yourself that perhaps relationship was a bit dangerous, that to share quite freely of the heart could bring challenge, could bring sorrow. And so you have encased the holy Child, the heart of you, in an armoring. You have said that, "It is only safe to share just so much of myself. Most of myself I will keep locked away until I am really sure that it's safe to open up." Now you are feeling a desire to throw off the encasement, as the seed does when it bursts forth with new life.

You have come through, even in this lifetime, numerous relationships, and there has been benefit in each one, even though at the time it might have felt a bit dubious, a bit sorrowful, a bit constricting. And yet at the vantage point where you find yourself now to be, you can look back upon all relationships and you can see where there has been love, true love and understanding, after you have been able to come past the behavior. And you have allowed yourself a bit of perspective, a bit of distance to look back upon it, and you have been able to see that that one, even though they may have been engaged in behavior which was not loving, was searching for Love. As you were.

Now there is a great desire to know love, unconditional unlimited Love — to come Home again by way of the avenue of extending, experiencing love. It is the grandest of gifts to give of your Self - the Self with a capital "S" — and in the giving, guess what happens? You find your Self. You experience your Self. As you allow the heart to open and to love freely — caring, understanding, asking only to be companion upon the path — as you allow the shutters of the heart to be flung wide open, you find your Self and you experience the Love which you have been searching for.

Falling in love is falling into a state of experiencing your Self, your true Self. For your true Self is most alive. Your true Self is most dynamically exhilarating. It is not the love as the world would teach you that has the conditions attached, the "shoulds" of how it can be extended, how it is safe, how it is not safe.

But your true Self is the exhilaration of falling in love. That is why it is so desired. For in those moments of falling in love you experience the releasing of the boundaries that you have thought yourself to be and the boundaries of what the world has taught you that love is.

The world has taught you that love is an exchange, that "I will give my love unto you if you give your love unto me," and/or "I will give my love unto you only if you give your love to me in a certain way." Not only that you give it, but that you give it in a certain way, perhaps in a long-term committed way, perhaps that you do not make waves, that you are always happy, that you find me to be the most wonderful person that you have ever met, and that you soothe my ego, et cetera. But that is not true love. That is conditional love.

That love you have known throughout aeons of time, and the conditions for that love have changed from culture to culture and society to society and time to time. That love changes, but the Love which you are is changeless. It abides forever. It goes beyond form. It goes beyond the physical exchange of energy known as form. When the form is laid down, the love does not end. The love that you carry in your heart for one is always there. No matter whether that one stand before you utilizing form or if that one stand before you in their Light body, the love that you carry in your heart for that one is always there, always alive, always eternal. And you experience why it feels so good to be in love, for you touch the eternal part of you.

What you are remembering is that the holy Child is the energy which activates form and even though the form be no longer with you, the Light that one is is always with you.

All of you have asked to know, what is love? For you have asked to know your Self. And you bring to yourself relationships, and the many forms of relationship, so that you can see beyond the limitation of form; so that you can look beyond the limitation of behavior, choices, personality; so that you can look beyond even the absence of form and feel the presence of Love nonetheless.

The presence of Love is very much where you are. The presence of Love is very much in your classroom, in your workplace, in your home, if you but have the eyes to see it — the eyes of the heart.

Falling in love is grand, and it can be done in every moment of every day. You can fall in love with the one who stands in front of you at your grocery store, the one who adds up all of what you are to pay in the golden coins, the one who runs each item across that beautiful window which measures, almost magically, what the items will cost.

You can fall in love with one that you see upon the street corner. You may never know their name in this lifetime. It matters not, for names change. You have known that one in other lifetimes. There is no one that you look upon that is a stranger to you.

Each and every one who stands before you is as a beautiful flower unfolding in their process. If you but take the time to pause and to look deeply with the eyes of the heart, you will fall in love.

This does not mean that it needs to be expressed in the ways of the world, for you have come past that. It needs to be expressed in the way of eternity, the way of unlimited Love, the way that says, "I recognize you. I see the Christ that you are. I look beyond the appearance and I see my Father in you."

And, in that, you fall in love every day.

Everyone who comes into your presence is as a beautiful gift you give unto yourself. For truly, beloved one, you have called them forth. They would not be there in your presence if you had not called them forth. And by the same token, they have called you forth in order to know and experience the Love that they are.

There are so many of your brothers and sisters who are still very much encased in their own shell. The seed is alive and well within them but the encasement is so dense that they are crying out to know hope, the possibility of Light, to have someone be outrageous enough to stand in front of them and to say, "Hi, how goes it with you today?" or even to say, "I feel lighter in the heart when I am with you." Every one of your brothers and sisters waits for your acknowledgment of Who they are. They wait for you to look them straight in the eye and to say, "I know Who you are."

Many of the brothers and sisters, as you have seen, go about with the eyes cast down. Many of them are so busy in what they think they are doing that they do not have time to pause and to behold the beauty of a sunrise or a sunset. Many of you have gone through lifetimes so afraid, so encased, that you have not even allowed yourself the hope that there could be love for you.

Many of the brothers and sisters you see now do not believe that another could look upon them and love them. And they do not love themselves for they are waiting to see it come from outside of themselves. They are waiting for someone else to recognize what they have not looked yet far enough to find within themselves, what they would not trust and do not trust.

And when you go about with a light heart, in love with life, guess what happens? It is contagious. Have you ever been around one who was in love? Yes, they get quite silly, and their energy is contagious. And I will share with you that that energy is your true nature and that is the energy which leads to ascension.

For as you have gone through what you would see as countless lifetimes dulled to the love of life, dulled to your own true nature, the very idea of ascension has been afar off. If you have heard of it at all in those lifetimes, it was that someone far removed from you, someone who had no relationship to you had ascended and must be worshipped as a god.

Now you are allowing yourself to contemplate the possibility, the probability and the truth of ascension. You are bringing forth a multitude of books, writings on ascension. You are bringing forth ones who give the workshops. You are bringing forth the guides and masters from what you still see as another place separate from you — and yet it is where you truly abide when the focus is expanded from this form and this expression — who will share with you what ascension is and what it feels like. And you are playing with the idea that perhaps, *perhaps*, ascension is possible for you. And it is.

For each and every one of you who has ever wondered about, played with the concept, looked upon a book about ascension, it is most possible, most probable that you will ascend even in what you see as this lifetime.

That is why you are calling it forth now in your consciousness. You have said at a very deep level, "I am ready to expand the boundaries of who I have thought myself to be. I am ready to welcome my unlimited Self and to know what that feels like." It is a grand time to be alive, for there is much that you will experience in what you see as this lifetime.

It is not just I, Jeshua ben Joseph, or other masters, cosmic and otherwise, who have ascended. I will share with you that you have ascended. Now, you say, "How can that be? I feel the body to be very much anchored right here."

I will share with you, first of all, that you have ascended; otherwise, you would not relate even to the concept. There is within you, at a very deep level, a knowing — a knowing of what ascension is all about. Where does that relatedness come from? Where does that knowingness come from? It comes from what we have described as the sphere of time — the sphere of the points of experience that you would label as lifetimes, histories, experiences of expression within the bubble of time — and within the bubble of time, as you see it to be, at least one of those points (and actually more) ascended.

Therefore, when we talk about ascension, there is a knowingness somewhere deep within you which says, "Yes, I can imagine what it would feel like to ascend." Somewhere within the bubble of all of the experiences of time you have ascended.

But let us bring it right here and now to what you know as this lifetime. Already you have ascended in moments when you felt yourself to be much more than what you thought yourself to be a moment previous. You have experienced moments of unlimitedness: in meditation perhaps, in music perhaps, in loving perhaps when you looked upon the small infant or beloved pet and you found yourself dissolved in love, unconditional and eternal, or when you have looked upon the sunset and you found yourself drawn into it. In that moment you have ascended. You forgot your close identification with this point of focus and you ascended.

In the days to come you will have more and more moments of ascension. You will find yourself not so anchored in the activities of the world and not so anchored in the identification with the body, and you will know that you have ascended for moments of time.

When you allow yourself to forget self — the small self — and you care for another, what they are feeling, what they are going through, and you are so identified with them that you feel you are actually inside their skin, looking out through their eyes, feeling their feelings, you have ascended and transcended the small personality.

In my lifetime I came to understand that I and the Father are one. I came to the place of knowing, with assurety, that I and the Father are one. There is no separation. I am Life upon this plane, as you are. I am Life upon this plane and all other planes and dimensions that you can ever imagine, will ever imagine, have ever imagined, and more.

I have collected unto myself the molecules of physicality in many, many forms. I played with, the same as you have, different forms of life expression upon this our Holy Mother, the Earth, and upon other planets and other universes as well, as you have done. For I am not limited and neither are you.

I and the Father are one. I am Life upon this plane, as you are. I am the Light which casts out all darkness. I am the Light which activates the form, as you are. The form, the body, what is it after you have chosen to lay it down? A lifeless form. You are not the body but you activate it. You use it for what you would see as a time interval. You are its master, although oftentimes it calls out to you and suggests that maybe it is the other way around. I experienced that, too.

Within what is known as life expression upon this plane there is first a descent into matter. You have chosen, as the god/Child that you are, to know what it feels like to be amongst your creations —not only to be amongst them but to activate them and to see what it feels like to go about with a density of form. And you have tried all kinds of forms. You have been the wooly mammoth. You have been the tiny songbird. You have been the eagle. You have been the dolphin. You have been the great whale. You have been the tiny minnow. You have been the alpine flower and the tallest sequoia tree. You have been all of those forms, and more.

I, too, have come many times to our Holy Mother, the Earth, to experience life with form. For I have enjoyed expressing creatively and knowing my creations. I have enjoyed relationship, true relationship of love extended and shared, as the simple peasant, the simple farmer, the simple fisherman. And I have also known lifetimes of complexity.

In the lifetime that is so famous now, the lifetime of Jeshua ben Joseph, I came with a purpose, as there is a purpose to your expression upon this plane. I came knowing the Light that I am, the Light that activated the small babe who was born, but I also experienced a close identification with form, for I desired to remember how it felt to be a man, to be human.

And so there was a period of time remembering what form is, what the body can do, and a time of experiencing all of the emotions which you experience — times of frustration when there were lessons set before me by my masters and I wrestled with those lessons and the answer did not come as quickly as I wanted it to, and I judged myself and I felt frustration; times when I looked upon another and I envied the form that that one was expressing with and I felt jealousy: until my earthly father, the one known as Joseph, sent me to sit by flowing water and to abide with myself —the small self — until I came into connection with my holy Self.

It was needful for me to go through a period of identification with what it means to be human so that I could intimately know how emotion, energy in motion, is experienced. Yes, I knew sorrow. In my human understanding I knew sorrow. For is it not written in your Scriptures that I was "a man of sorrows, and acquainted with grief"? (I was also a man of laughter, and acquainted with joy.) And when I allowed myself the perspective of the whole vision, the holy vision, there was no longer sorrow. For there is only sorrow when it is measured within the limited framework of time. Outside of time it matters not, for the holy Child abides always within the Kingdom of our Father. However, within the bubble of time, within the bubble of the experience known as lifetimes, there can be sorrow because of the identification with form and its potential for loss, and because of the belief in the gradations of values, as seen in time.

In the unfoldment of my remembrance I knew sorrow. And I knew human love. I knew attraction of form to form, physical attraction. I looked upon ones who utilized the form of woman, and beheld them as beautiful. And there were ones who stirred my heart as a man. There were ones who had the dancing eyes, who gave my heart opportunity to flip. And it did.

I knew the feelings of human love, but there was within me, as there is within you, a very deep knowing that there is more. I knew that there was an integration of wholeness, a balance, if you will, where all of what I experienced as a human was seen within the whole of experience, and I knew that which is beyond human love. I knew that there is eternal love which goes beyond form no matter how beautiful the form.

For indeed, the spirit is what you fall in love with. It is not the form — although the packaging may be what attracts you at first. Packaging can be beautiful. But as you abide with that one and you look beyond the packaging, what you fall in love with is your Self. You fall in love with the higher attributes of your Self. You fall in love with Love Itself.

Falling in love has much to do with ascending in love. Descending into the experience of matter, of form, has much to do with ascending. For now you are in the process of knowing, consciously knowing, the marriage of energy — of Light energy called Spirit — and form, which is light taken into a density acknowledged as form.

You are coming to a conscious awareness of an integration, a marriage, knowing that, "I walk. I activate form. I activate it as a vehicle of expression that speaks a language unto the brothers and sisters who understand the language of the body, of physicality.

But I am much more than the form. I am the energy that activates that form, and in that awareness I come totally alive."

It does not mean that you have to lay down the form to ascend. It does not mean that you have to die in order to live. What you are asking now and what you will experience in love, true love, is the marriage of Who you are as Light, with your creation of light, otherwise known as form.

In that, beloved one, you are married unto all you see. Everyone. Even the ones that perhaps you would rather they went somewhere else. Hmmm. And with the other ones that your heart goes out to. You are married to every one and every thing you see.

You are the energy of Spirit. You are the energy of life. You are the energy of Light that even now your scientists are coming to measure. You are the energy which activates every form you see, and gives life to every event, every circumstance, every relationship. Then you come to the place of saying, "Yes, Father, I am your Life upon this plane, and I enjoy life" — for *He* does — not the activity of the world, but Life.

In my lifetime, because I knew my oneness with the very Life energy that we are, I came unto a place of knowing that I no longer needed a special time to speak to my Father, as in prayer. I no longer needed a specific time for the communion of oneness as in meditation, for I knew myself to be at every moment the Life of the Father upon this plane. I knew myself to be, in every moment, one as His energy. And in that instant of true knowing, that instant of coming Home, the very cells of the body took on a radiance which has been called in your Scriptures the Transfiguration.

There were ones of my friends, known as disciples — and it was not just the men disciples; there were women as well — who witnessed what has been called the Transfiguration. They witnessed that moment in time, for yes, it was in time, when I so knew the energy that I am that the very cells themselves came alive with Light. There was yet form to be seen, but it was transfigured as the Light that activates the form. I was a bit surprised. It was not something that I had as a conscious goal. In fact, I did not know that would happen.

And after the crucifixion and the resurrection, it was my great joy to reunite with many of you again, utilizing the body. I appeared to you in the Upper Room, which surprised you a bit, and spent many days with you teaching, supporting, strengthening. For you already knew much of what I had been teaching — it had been received within the heart — but there needed to be an integration, a firing such as you will see with a gemstone: when it is put to the fire, then comes the brilliance. I knew that the fire would be there for you and that you would come to remember the brilliance of your Light.

Because you had witnessed the transfiguration, because you had witnessed the resurrection, which seemed most miraculous, you were open to understanding that there might be even more. There was much that we shared.

And then, in the fullness of time, there was another demonstration, the demonstration known as the ascension, in which I allowed myself to be so filled with the Love — the unlimited unconditional exhilarating Love; dynamic, forceful, powerful Love — that the very cells themselves could no longer be held upon this plane. And in Light I was seen to ascend. And you will do so, if it is your desire.

It is not necessary that one ascend in that manner in order to be worthy to know the Love of the Father. There are some who will choose that activity again *in conscious awareness*, and others who will lay down the dust of the body and go as the Light being that they are without the demonstration of the ascension. For it is not necessary.

The ascension that *is* necessary is the one that you are in process of claiming right now: the ascension of consciousness, the ascension that says, "I know that I am the Spirit, the Light, that activates all of form. I know that I am my Father's creative Child, for I am the Child of the Creator. How could I not be creative?" And you are very creative. Now you are desiring to know creativity in joy — no longer creativity in confusion and sorrow, in conflict. You know that very well. Now you are choosing to know your creativity in joy, in love.

Ascension is not difficult. Ascension is not something that has to be done in a certain ritual with much help from many masters. You are a master yourself. Ascension is not something that is complex.

Now, you may make it seem complex — and you have. You have written the classic works on the subject. You have described the various levels of purification, all of the requirements. You have been the priest and priestess who has decreed yourself to be the authority, who has said that ascension is only for one who is very God, perhaps masters who have come through stages of enlightenment, and only for ones who would be worshipped as greatly above you. You have written, and you have studied, all of the authoritative books.

But ascension, beloved one, is simplicity itself. It is allowing yourself to come beyond the specific point of focus and to expand into the totality of aliveness, into the totality of Love. Begin by falling in love with life, with choices, with adventure. Say, "Yes, I will live each moment totally and truly alive in Love." And then there is ascension.

And once you have ascended — and you have — you can do it again and again and again until there is no longer the need or desire to be identified with this form. You will identify with the Light form that you are, and then you will go beyond even that to know the consciousness of Allness.

You will know yourself to be the I Am which abides forever.

The Days To Come

Beloved one, I would share with you a new prophecy. You have heard it said that the days to come will be hard times, times of sorrow, upheaval, doom and gloom. And many there are of your brothers and sisters who will look upon events and judge them, from habitual perception, to be of tragedy. But I say unto you that is not my message. That is not my gospel. My gospel is one of good news and it concerns not just one Jeshua ben Joseph, one personification of the Christ, for indeed I behold the Christ of you, as you read these words.

My gospel is that the days to come are times of joy; times of fulfillment; times of enlightenment. It is not by accident that you have heard that you are ushering in an age of enlightenment, for indeed you are. You have decreed that you will know the Light; that you will allow the heaviness of the world to be dead and buried, and that you will resurrect the remembrance of a light heart. And in that you are enlightened.

Enlightenment begins with a willingness — a willingness to relax the habitual constraints of judgment, to open the shutters of the heart, to see with new eyes each and every one who stands before you, each and every thing which you behold in creation. It is a willingness to play with concepts of the mind, to play with possibilities, to read books which are exciting, uplifting and inspiring, which will suggest something beyond what the world believes the boundaries of truth to be. Your works of what would be called fiction, the works called scientific fiction, allow you to go beyond the bounds of what you have thought yourself to be and what you have thought the possibilities to be. That is why you play with those ideas. For indeed it allows an awakening within one's self to say, "Perhaps, perhaps I am more than what society has taught me I am. Perhaps I am more than what the parents have taught me I am. Perhaps I am more than what my co-workers and my peers have said that I am. Perhaps I am free to go where no man yet has gone. To boldly go." And you play with ideas of unlimitedness.

As you allow the expansion of unlimitedness to come into your conscious awareness, to live it, to feel it even within the very cells of the body, you come alive and enlightenment begins —literally.

You are the adventurer, the pioneer, the one who says, "What more is there? What new land can I conquer? What new idea can I play with and where will this idea take me?" For indeed, as you start with one idea, it begins a train of thought which takes you beyond wherever you thought you might go. And as you have the willingness to release limitation of belief, you play with the possibility that perhaps the days to come can be ones of fulfillment.

Yes, there will be the upheavals: the upheavals in the sense of the physicalness of change in our holy Mother, the Earth, *and* the upheavals within the belief system. For indeed you will be releasing limited beliefs about yourself, about the brothers and sisters, and about what the world is for. Even with regard to the physical upheavals, you are saying, "Perhaps, perhaps I am strong enough to play with the idea that there can be upheaval and I as the Christ that I am will come through all of that. I will endure." For indeed you will. You are eternal. You are the Light that cannot be hindered, and there is nothing that will come nigh your temple that will threaten you.

There will be changes, yes. There are changes in the days to come. And there are many who will look upon those changes and will say, "Woe is me. This is the prophecy that has been foretold. This is the doom that I have expected," and for them they will see events that way.

There will be others of the brothers and sisters, ones who have witnessed events that the world would judge to be tragic — perhaps they have lost all of the material possessions — and they have had opportunity to stand in a moment and to ask, "What is important?" And they have said, "I and my family have survived. We have endured. That is what is important. We can rebuild the structure of the house. We can collect again the material possessions." You have heard some in recent times say that. And they have come unto a revelation that what matters is not the physical, not the material possessions, not even, if you will receive it, the physical form, for they have had opportunity to know the ongoingness of the Light that they are. Many have called forth events which are judged as tragic in order to have opportunity to clear away all of the dust, all of the chaos of world beliefs, and to come unto their own place of knowing what is Truth.

Some of the brothers and sisters have bemoaned because the material possessions have been lost. They will have again the opportunity to stand upon the threshold of knowing Who they are. Not because masters outside of themselves or a God afar off is going to cause events as a punishment. No, it is because they will call forth one more opportunity to come through the event to know the Truth of their being.

In the days to come, there will be upheaval, there will be shifts, there will be changes in the very topography of our Holy Mother, the Earth. But so what. This is not the first lifetime that you have ridden the roller coaster of changes of topography. It is not the first lifetime that you have looked upon the mountain that would spew forth its energy. All of you as the adventurers that you are have experienced laying down the body through events of nature, as it is called. It is not a nature outside of yourself; it is your own nature that you are calling forth. And if it be your own nature — and I assure you that it is — what does that say about you, grand adventurer that you are?

The days to come are ones of great joy. They are a time of opportunity to come unto a clarity of heart, to know, not just in words, in intellectual concepts, but to know as a Truth of your being that you are more than the events that are happening. And you will find yourself in joy even though all of the circumstances around you may be having their upheavals and their fallings down. You will feel a joy, an inexplicable joy — inexplicable in the world's terms — as you keep your mind and your heart centered upon Who you are, upon the Christ that you are.

Now, I do not mean to speak here of physical events of our Holy Mother, the Earth, in a way that you will say, "Uh, oh; he's giving a prediction. I have to be prepared to protect myself." That is not my message. My message is that yes, there will be the changes, for indeed there have always been changes, and it is not that you have to run anywhere to be safe. You are safe wherever you are.

My message is one of great joy. For you have de-creed at a very deep level that you will come Home again, that you will know in conscious awareness the power of the Light that you are. You will do what is necessary in terms of sustaining the body, and there may be guidance to help others if they need some of the material possessions, a roof over the head, a bed, food. You will share. But more than that, you will share of the peace that comes from the strength of your knowing.

As you play with the possibility that the days to come can be times of great joy, as you allow yourself to abide in the heart with the love and the peace that comes from entertaining that concept, there comes a feeling of probability. "Well, probably if X, Y, and Z happen, I'll come through them. I'll be okay." And this is a grand Truth.

Where does that knowing come from? It comes from a place deep within that the world and the voice of the ego will question, very much as you would see a jousting match. The voice of the ego will clamor for attention, with its questions and its doubts. But yet there abideth the still small Voice that says, "I will come through this for I am my Father's Child."

The days to come are ones of great healing: healing of physical form if that need be, but more than that, they will be days of great healing where you know your wholeness as the totality of Self, where it matters not what the form will do or will not do, for the energy of Light that activates the form is not contained within the form, and cannot be contained by any limitation.

There were times in my lifetime when I heard the voice of ego, but I also heard the Voice of my Father, Who said, "If you are Life —and you are — you are more than form. You are more than what the mind would tell you that you are. If you are Life — and I assure you that you are — you are more than the small point of focus known as one form, one personality in one lifetime."

When I came unto the evening before what you now call Good Friday, and I went unto the garden in Gethsemane, the voice of ego came again, for it was my companion, as it is yours. And I asked of my Father if there were another way to fulfill the service that I knew I had come to do. Could we let this cup pass from me? In other words, "Father, can we think of plan B? Surely there must be another way we can do this." And then the still small Voice, which speaks so loudly when you allow the dust of the world to settle, arose within me and said, "I and the Father are one. I do the will of my Father, for I am one with Him. I am Life. And if the form be laid down, the Life that I am will abide." And I rested in the peace of that knowing.

All of you have agreed that you will come to a certain point of focus known as this lifetime, and you will pick up a script and you will be as the grand actor upon the stage. And there are times when you get very much into your role and you act it with great emotion — emotion that can be heard to the farthest universes. And there is nothing wrong with that. You are playing your part; that is exactly what you are doing. You are playing — but sometimes that aspect of it is forgotten. You have all agreed to a certain collective script, to begin with, and then you have written into that agreement a clause that says, "From this point on I will develop my abilities in improv. I will in each moment be free to choose. There is no delineation of character that *has* to be. I will form the character of this part as I go along." And you do this.

For the one that you would see yourself to be right now is very different from the one that you would perceive as expressing a year ago, or ten years ago. And it is because of choices you have allowed yourself to make; it is because of the clause you put in the agreement that says, "I am open to improvisation, and I will become a master of improv." And in every moment you are free to choose anew.

And as you choose anew, what happens to all of the rest of the actors on the stage? They have to choose anew because you've changed the script. So you see how interrelated you are? There is no separation. For as one chooses to awaken, he changes the script of everyone else, and everyone else has to adjust a bit. It is called a dance: as you choose anew, everything else shifts. As you choose for the higher knowing, for the expanded understanding, for ascension, all of creation is lifted up. "I, if I be lifted up, will draw all men unto me."

Now, I did not mean that as I, Jeshua ben Joseph, as a personality, an individual, if I be lifted up, I will draw all men unto me. I meant that if I, in my awareness and awakening as the Christ that I am, be lifted up, in that revelation I will draw all men unto me, for everything has to shift and adjust in the improv. That is what that statement means, and that is what happens when each and every one of you chooses anew for Love, for remembrance.

In the days to come you will awaken and you will know the Love that you are, the unassailable Love that you are — even while expressing with the form of the body, if that is your desire. For it is not necessary to lay down the body to go unto a place called Heaven. Many, many, many times you have laid down the body in a belief taught unto you by your priests and priestesses, taught unto you by the so-called learned ones, that once you were out of this vale of sorrows, having laid down the body, instantly everything would be beautiful and wonderful.

And so when you came unto what you would see as the end of the time interval known as that lifetime, and you laid down the body, if your belief system was that you would go unto a place where the angels would sing, then you have experienced the heaven of your belief. Then there has been a feeling, a desire within you, that, "Perhaps there is still yet something I haven't experienced," and you have chosen to focus and express again — with different form perhaps, or different culture — for the fun of it.

The days to come will be a time when you will consciously anchor your Light upon this plane in your remembrance of the totality of Light that you are, so that others may have opportunity to remember the Light that they are. You are all as great beacons; the Light that you are cannot be hid. Even in moments when you, in your own self-image, would want to put the bushel over yourself and to hide your Light, all you do is a temporary hiding of the Light from yourself. You are as a great Light that is set upon the hill and cannot be hid.

The days to come are grand times, exciting times. Be of good cheer for my gospel is your gospel. It is the good news of the days to come. And, if you will receive it, where are those days? Right here. Right now. You are amongst those days. It is not something that you need wait for. You do not need to wait until I would descend in a beautiful chariot of Light, surrounded by the angels proclaiming the coming of Christ. That happens in your heart whenever you allow the peace of the Father full conscious expression.

I have been asked if the Second Coming will be as it has been prophesied: will I come from the Heavens in a grand chariot of Light with the angels? Yes, I will — for some of the brothers and sisters, for that is what they have decreed is necessary and that is what they will manifest.

For others of you that is not necessary, for you have already found the awakening within your own heart, within your own Self. Will you see me descend from Heaven in a great radiance of Light? If you desire to. Anytime you look unto your heavens and you behold the beauty of the clouds — the chariot of a cloud — and your heart opens in joy, where am I then?

That is what the days to come are all about for you and for others who have the eyes to see with joy and the ears to hear the angelic singing, the singing that is truly your heart expressing. Do the angels sing? Of course they do.

You, as you express right now in what is a seeming individuality, a coalescence of the Light, you are a vibration. The energy is a vibration, and, if you could hear, there is a grand chorus of vibration, for you are joined by others you would call the Light beings and the angels. You are in a sea of beingness, the One that you are. And yes, there is an angelic chorus.

And if you have the ears of the heart to hear it, it is most joyous. If you have the ears of the world you will hear discord. But now you are into improv, and much joy will it bring you. That is what the days to come are all about: joy; fulfillment —fulfillment of the desire that you expressed even before time began — enlightenment, for you will know the Light that you are even as you express with the form — transformation and remembrance.

Be of good cheer. Be of Light heart — for that is truly Who you are — and spread the gospel. Not the gospel of one who lived many, many years ago, but your own gospel: the Truth of your being. It is good news. It is joy. And as you allow yourself to abide in that joy, know that the days to come will be as *you* decree.

Manifesting Heaven on Earth

Beloved one, let us speak now about a topic which is dear to my heart — and yours as well — a topic which you have invited me to discuss, to commune with you about, for indeed it is a desire of your heart to see Heaven manifest upon Earth and to know once again what you remember at a very deep level. You remember Home, you remember Heaven, and there is a very strong desire arising now within the holy Child to see it manifest upon this plane.

You desire to see the beauty of Light once again as it was in the beginning, even upon our holy Mother, the Earth, and to behold the animals, the birds, the friends and companions in oneness again. You desire to behold once again the flowers, the trees, the abundance of vegetation surrounded and activated by the Light of creation, as you knew in the beginning. You desire to see all things anew.

You have asked to behold once again beauty in all of form, to behold radiance, and to bring forth all that Heaven is, all that you remember Home to be, and to experience it and to share it with the brothers and sisters while still activating form, no longer to believe that you have to lay down the body and go unto a far place in order to know Heaven, for indeed you have done that countless times. You have raised up a body and you have expressed with the body until you have gotten tired — tired not so much of the body but tired in the spirit, holding an imperfect image of self — and you have laid down that body, hoping that you would go unto Heaven forever and ever — and you have. You have gone unto what your belief system foretold after laying down the body, and after a while you have chosen to raise up a new form, human or otherwise.

Now you are desiring to know Heaven right here, to bring the totality of Home to this plane, to know Love, to see it expressed in harmony between brother and sister, sister and sister, brother and brother, between all life forms, and to behold the great radiance of that Love.

What is coming in your days to come need not be a time of doom and gloom. There have been prophecies of such, and some of the brothers and sisters have accepted such prophecy and have said, "This is how it must be." And for them, indeed, there will be some of the upheavals, some of what they will see as trage- dies, for they have decreed that that is necessary before they come to a place of worthiness to accept what is already theirs: to accept and to claim Heaven. But you may — indeed, you must — come to know Heaven in gentleness.

Now, some have asked me, "Well, Jeshua, if we were to bring Heaven to Earth, would it not blow all of the circuits?" And indeed it will blow the circuits of the limitation of belief and the limitation of image, for your understanding of yourself will go beyond what has been known and accepted for a long, long time.

But you have decreed at a very deep level that you are willing to know your totality and to express the Light that you are in radiant form, in love, in free- dom, in joy upon this plane. And that is what your days to come are all about.

For indeed in every moment you decree what you are going to experience. You call it forth, and then, as the habit of mankind/womankind has been, you sit in judgment of it, seeing it as either good or, more often, as lacking in something and not quite what you would like to experience. And yet it is exactly what you have asked to experience in order to see the blessing of it.

You call forth everything that you experience, not as a judgment sent by a Father afar off or by masters who would say that you need to learn something or that you are not quite good enough yet, so therefore you have to come through certain tests and trials. That is not it at all. You call it forth yourself in order to know your holiness, in order to know your wholeness, the totality of Who you are, and to claim what you have previously seen to be separate aspects of yourself, to experience them and to integrate them into your awareness of the wholeness that you are.

So whatever you experience, whatever you call forth, abide with it in the heart, in peace, and ask of it, "What message do you have for me? Where is the Heaven in this?" For indeed, Heaven is not afar off. Heaven is right where you are this moment, and *every* moment, as you choose to see it with the eyes of the heart.

Many lifetimes you have had philosophies, theologies, which would explain in great detail what Heaven is and how to reach Heaven. And many lifetimes your ones in authority known as the priests — or by whatever name they have been called — have told you that there is much of study, much of ritual, much of cleansing, much of purification, many trials to come through before you would be worthy to know Heaven.

And you as the holy Child, you have said, "Okay, I will experience this. I will say that Heaven is somewhere a bit distant from me, so that I can experience how it feels to be outside of the Kingdom, outside of Heaven." And there has been no judgment by the Father of His holy Child, for the Child, being creative of nature, has dreamed many dreams and has listened to many stories — and has even given forth many stories.

For you as priest/priestess in what you would know as other lifetimes have given forth much advice to the brothers and sisters as to how to attain a state of worthiness so that when the body was released the Father would accept you back into His house.

Well, beloved one, you have never gone from the Father's mansion. You have experienced many rooms in the Father's mansion — this is but one of them — but you have never gone from the Father's Kingdom, and you have never gone from Heaven except as you have chosen to turn the focus of your attention unto what you would call and judge to be other than Heaven. For Heaven is right with you. It is within and you carry it with you, as You, wherever you go.

So it is not what you would see as a complex task to manifest Heaven on Earth, although it would be called a miracle. The miracle lies in the willingness to abide every moment in the peace of the heart and to look upon everything that transpires with the eyes of Love, with the eyes that say, "There must be a holiness, a wholeness of vision." And if you do not see it at first, ask to see with the eyes of the Father.

The days to come are ones of Heaven upon Earth, for you have decreed that you have tried all of the other ways of experiencing and expressing, and you have tired, as a child does of toys that are outgrown, of the many different ways of knowing your creativity. Now you are saying, "Father, I want to return as the prodigal Son/Daughter that I am. I want to return to my Father's House, and I want to remember Home in such dynamic expression, visible upon this plane, that all of the brothers and sisters who so choose may also witness and be part of the experience of Heaven."

What you behold as yet is but a fraction of the Light that is radiating all around you as you. You have hints, you have clues; ones have seen the auras of Light around the form. You have seen the body that is laid down, the lifeless body, and you have seen that there is something missing: the body lying there, the raiment that you put on for a lifetime, is not activated by energy.

What you are willing to do now is to bring more and more of the Light that you are into visibility, into the very cells of the body, to allow more and more of the Light to radiate so that it will be seen visibly even with the physical eyes.

Already you have experienced the energy of brothers and sisters, for you have been in a group of people and you have seen one who was feeling a bit dejected, confused perhaps, a lot on the mind, weight upon the shoulders. And you have felt a heaviness of energy with that one.

And, you have been in a group where one has come in and has been most elated, most excited about something. You have a term for this: it is called, "turned on." Their Light is turned on and it is visible. You can actually see the Light around that one. You can see the love light in the eyes. You can feel the Light of the heart. You can feel the vibration which comes from that one. It is no longer a vibration that is held very close to the form but it is a vibration which fills the whole room, and everyone in the room feels and has opportunity to be uplifted by that energy.

More and more you will be allowing the Light that you are, the Light that activates the form, to be visible. No longer will the belief in separation be tenable, because you will see the light of one intermingling with the light of another and another. You will see the light fill all of space, and you will not be able to say that you are separate one from another, for "your" light will be in their space, and vice versa: "their" light will fill your space.

No longer will ones be able to say the body is the boundary and that there is separation between ones.

You have already experienced having an idea or a thought, contemplating it in "your" mind, and one close to you has started to speak about the same topic. And you have said, "How did you know I was thinking about that?" They knew what you were thinking for there is no separation.

It is bodies that appear to be separate, but the energy that you are, the Light that you are, the Thought that you are is one. There is no separation, even with brothers and sisters who would seem to be at a distant geographical location. As you hold that one in your heart and as you think upon them, even though they be what you would see as miles away, they feel your love and your caring. And oftentimes the telephone will ring, and there that one will be speaking to you. There is no separation.

Heaven upon Earth will be the most visible manifestation of oneness. You will know yourself to be one with all of creation. It will be most visible. You will know yourself to be one with the flowers that grow. You will sit, as you can do now, with a flower, and you can hear it unfolding. You can speak to the flower and ask the plant, the blade of grass, to share with you its story. And as you listen, you will hear a wondrous story that is not separate from you, for it is your story as well.

All of what you have brought forth on the face of our holy Mother, the Earth, is beautiful. It is there to remind you of your beauty and your oneness. And the time comes rapidly now, for you who are of like mind and for the brothers and sisters who are yet awakening, when there will be known that there is no separation. For even the ones who go about now in sorrow and in great confusion and in what you would call violence and conflict are calling out to know that they are loved and that they are Love.

You have known much of relationship based on the belief in separation, where ones have believed that they could act from a place of not knowing oneness with the brothers and sisters and that they could act with impunity.

And yet they have enacted the drama in order to know that they are not separate from the brothers and sisters who have agreed to be servants, one unto the other, so that the brothers living in the belief in separation have opportunity to experience and know and come Home once again.

If you will receive it, the ones who have laid down the body in violence have agreed that they would do so as servants for all of the brothers and sisters. And your heart has gone out to support the ones who are going through a seeming loss. If you will receive it, the events known as the bombing in Oklahoma City and the later destruction of the World Trade Center towers in your New (York) City are part of manifesting Heaven on Earth. Now, there are many in your world who would not understand that statement and would say that that is heresy. "What does he mean by that?"

What I mean by that, is that there has been opportunity to look past the appearance of tragedy. You have allowed the heart to open, and you have witnessed a growing number of the brothers and sisters also opening the heart and extending support in many, many different ways. And you have looked upon these events with new eyes. Even what you call your press, your media, have reported on the selfless acts of love extended, rather than completely looking upon what has been judged to be bad. There is much of Heaven that is being manifest even through seeming tragedy.

As you allow yourself to abide in the heart with whatever experience comes to your consciousness, whatever experience you call forth, and ask to see Heaven even through seeming tragedy, you manifest Heaven on Earth in that moment. Are you willing to look for Heaven? You will find it.

For long enough has mankind/womankind looked upon the side of tragedy and separation, limitation and judgment of self and others. Now as you are willing to look for the love that is in your experience, you will call forth more and more of that love. For indeed, whatever you shine the Light of your countenance upon grows, as the tiny plant grows in the sunshine. Whatever you focus upon is what increases in your experience.

Therefore, choose you Heaven. As you do that moment by moment, all of creation rearranges itself to accede to your desire. How could it not? You are the one who is calling forth creation. As you have what is called a change of heart, creation changes and you behold miracles. Does it in fact change? Yes. It changes in your perception and it changes in truth — with a small "t" — for the truth is the truth of your dream. And no longer is there need to experience the unhappy dream. You have tried that over and over and you know it intimately. You have experienced the dream of sorrow and lack and limitation. You have experienced the dream of violence, brother against brother. You have experienced the dream that has been as the nightmare, and now you are saying, "I will awake. I will arise and go again unto my Father's House. I will live the Adventure awake."

All of creation will mirror Heaven back to you as you are willing to abide in the heart of Love and to look upon everything in holiness. Is this a miracle? Yes. The miracle is in the willingness of choosing. For the keys to bringing forth Heaven upon this plane begin with the desire to experience Heaven once again, to know it right here. That is what you have desired to do and it is what you have agreed to do even from the point of the beginning of time. You have desired to come to the experience of physicality and to anchor your Light upon this plane, and, in the anchoring, to realize Heaven upon Earth. The desire is very true and very real.

You now are at the place of intention, the second key of manifesting Heaven. You have said, "I intend to know Heaven right where I am. No longer will I feel that it is necessary to lay down the body and escape this experience in order to know Heaven. I will put it off no longer. I intend to bring Heaven to a conscious realization right here and right now."

And then you allow it to be seen, for the third key is one of allowance. In faith and allowance you rest. You allow Heaven to come into your awareness and you look for it amidst all of the other appearances.

The fourth key is one of surrender in knowing you have received. You no longer feel that you must make it happen. You surrender into the knowingness that it has already been with you, as You, all the time. It requires no great complexity: you surrender to what has always been. You are your Father's holy Child; you are the peace that you seek. You are the Heaven you would manifest.

Bring forth now the deep abiding Peace of the Father, the beauty of Heaven. Know Love in all you behold. It is time. It is time because you have decreed that it is time. You are responding to your own wake-up call. You are responding to the very deep longing within the heart to know the peace and the Love that you remember.

For, as I speak these words, there is a remembrance. You remember what Heaven feels like. You have experienced and expressed Heaven upon this plane, and you desire now to return once again to what you remember.

Heaven is gentleness. Heaven is the strength of gentleness.

Heaven is Love, and you have felt Love for one another. The Love of the Father is unfathomable by the mind but it is known in the heart. It is what comes forth in the tears of oneness. It is expressed through the eyes that look upon another one and no longer see separation or difference, but only see the oneness of understanding.

That is Heaven, and it is here and it is now. It can be no other place, for Heaven is right where you are. And it can be no other time, for there is only the now moment. Every moment that you experience is, at that moment, now.

Heaven is the truth of your Reality and it comes forth whenever you desire to know it. It is within your heart. It is within you. It is closer than hands or feet; closer than breathing, for breath is of the body. Heaven is of the Spirit.

Heaven is the peace of trusting in what is unseen and unknown. Heaven is the peace that passes the understanding of the world. Heaven is the hope of the vision that you hold within your heart. Allow yourself to remember that you are Heaven upon this plane, and each time you look into the eyes of a brother or sister, each time you look into the eyes of a beloved pet, a companion upon the journey, and you behold the one Self, you manifest Heaven in that moment.

Heaven is the simplicity of saying, "I have arrived. I am Home. I am holy. I am whole. I am the Love that I seek."

Are you willing to look for Heaven? You will find it.

The Age of Enlightenment:
The Remembrance of Innocence

Beloved one, oftentimes you have ushered in a new age. This is not the first time that you have participated in the turning of the age, and the remembrance comes from deep within that says, "Yes, somehow I know the subtlety of anticipation of things to come, a suggestion that there is much more to the experience upon this plane than just what appearance would show." In times past, you have searched your holy books, you have gone to your teachers, your rabbis, the masters, and you have said, "Share with me your secrets," and they have.

And you have brought forth from your own inner wisdom the revelations which you have shared with your disciples, and the revelations and the teachings based on those revelations have been handed down from generation to generation. You have written the books, known as classics, which have within them the squiggles that are the symbols of remembrance, for indeed the squiggles on the page mean nothing except as *you* give them meaning and they serve as your catalyst for remembrance.

There has been much written — and many workshops given — within recent time facilitating communication with the inner child, allowing the child to express. For indeed as you re-establish an awareness of the child within, you begin to remember the holy Child that you are, and great is the rejoicing that comes forth from the remembrance.

For long enough have you acquiesced to the voice of the world that has constricted the expression of the child. Long enough have you hidden deep within yourself the Child that you are. Now you are finding reasons to celebrate, to laugh, to love, to hope, to play with each other. And when you do that, you touch the place of the Child. You touch the place of Heaven and bring it to Earth.

Your days to come are days of innocence, remembering again what would seemingly be a long time ago — and yet it is but the twinkling of an eye — when you first chose to express upon our Holy Mother, the

Earth, remembering the beauty that you beheld in our creations. You are allowing yourself now to pause, to look upon the beauty of our Holy Mother, the Earth, in communion with the flowing waters, the softness of the gentle rains, the caress of the wind, the warmth of the sun as it nurtures the process of life.

Your days to come are days of enlightenment, for you have decreed that you will choose the Lighter path. Your enlightenment comes as you are willing to look upon everything that you have created and to call it good. For long enough has mankind/womankind looked upon his/her creations and judged them to be less than perfect. Now is the time when you are choosing to look upon all of your creations, not only the ones in physical form but also your creations as relationships, circumstances and events that you experience, and to call them good even as you are in the midst of what the ego would judge to be confusing, sorrowful, not quite perfect. And yet everything which you call forth is perfect, for you have decreed that you will bring it forth in order to know its holiness and to come through it to remembering your own holiness.

The days to come, beloved one, are days of Light, days of beauty, days of joy, days of upliftment, days of unlimited Love — not only knowing love in human relationships as they have been defined for so long, but knowing the joy of relationship which is unlimited, the relationship of One.

Many of the brothers and sisters are choosing to know continuing relationship which goes beyond the form of the body. Many are laying down the body and will choose to recycle, as it is called, to be born of woman again as you have done many, many times, and you will see them again as the small ones, the infants. And you will say, "I know I know that one." And you do. Others are choosing to know new expression as the Light which they are, and in that power of Light will manifest the light body in ways that you can remember but have not witnessed for some time. It will seem to be miraculous and yet, as it happens, you will remember that you have done this.

There will be many miracles in the days to come. Your press, your media, are going to be most busy. At first there will be the skepticism; you are seeing the first wave of this. There will be skepticism and there will be the ones sent out to research the occurrence to see if it could be true. And there will be ones who, because of belief born of many lifetimes, will feel that it serves them well to be in a place of power to say that this life is the only way it can be, and that it is a sin to think otherwise. Oftentimes you have known constraint by dictate of limited belief.

But now you are arising, saying, "No longer. I will experience my unlimitedness, the Love that is eternal, and I will experience my Father's house — not only upon this plane, but in all other planes of expression." And you are calling forth, because of the energy that you are and the ones that you are not separate from, "proof," as it will be seen, that there is much more to life expression than what has been known in limited form.

You will see miraculous healings, instantaneous healings, as ones accept their worthiness to know that they are whole. They will no longer see it necessary to suffer in order to go unto a place where they will be perfect, as in Heaven. But they will know their holiness even in expression, and the resultant joy is most contagious.

You will see ones arising from the dead — ones who have laid down the body rising up again. It will be seen as miraculous. But even more miraculous than that is the arising from the dead in spirit, from the place that says, "Life is not worth living. There is no joy, and I don't know why I'm here." What is most miraculous is the willingness to arise up in consciousness, claiming again the power of your beingness, the power through which you have called forth all of your creations which serve you well.

You will see Light beings as light beings. You will know your oneness with what are called the angels. You have seen a resurgence of interest in angels, for many are playing with the possibility that an angel could very much be in your midst. And she is.

You will come to know the communion of angels, and you will experience communing with loved ones who have laid down the body and have found, to their great amazement sometimes, that they are still alive. They come and knock upon the door of your heart and mind, and they say, "I want to talk with you. I am still alive. I have found joy."

Even the process that has been accepted as inevitable, the process of aging as it is called, does not have to happen. You have seen ones — and you will see more and more — reversing the process of aging, reversing it because there has been a belief that it had to progress in a certain manner and now they are decreeing youth. You will see them expressing in great wholeness, health, vitality. You will see others laying down the body because they feel it is finished, but they know themselves very much to be alive and they will be right back with you again, no longer needing to come through a process, unless they so choose, of allowing the body to grow in stature. They will manifest the full-grown body.

You will see the ones of the animals also resurrecting themselves, for in life essence they are no different from you and the brothers and sisters. You will see the animals that you now hold to be in mythology coming to be in your experience once again, to play with you as they have done in what you would call olden times. They are very much alive and well, just awaiting your invitation to come. They are in the wings, waiting their time to come and play their script again. To play — to play, that is the secret.

In your days to come you will be bringing forth more and more of technology to serve you. You will not see yourself to be separate from technology, for you will know that as you bring forth the equipment, the gadgetry, it is you as the creative master who calls it forth for the purpose of knowing your creative unlimitedness.

Know you that is why you now have what are called the computers? The so-called "artificial" intelligence is an extension of the one Mind that you are, symbolic and catalytic for your remembrance of All that you are.

You are calling forth technology in many forms which will allow you to measure and to prove the energy that you are, energy that will allow you to go unto the dimensions you desire to travel unto.

You are bringing forth the technology of sound which will allow the balancing of the vibration of the body. You are bringing forth the technology of color — which you have worked with in other lifetimes — to heal. Many times in what you would see as long ago, you had rooms filled with the light of certain colors, and you were one who could look upon a form to behold which chakras were free-flowing in the energy patterns and which ones had closed down. And you knew, not by the outer sight but by the inner sight, what vibration would be balancing. You used vibration of sound and color to balance and restore the energy flow of the body. And now you are playing with new technology utilizing vibration for healing.

With regard to collective groupings known as countries you will behold miracles in the days to come. You will see ones who are in a place of calling forth their power, as they know the power of the world to be, who will motivate others to be in conflict, brother against brother. You will see ones coming together into great armies for they feel that there is not a choice, that they must do this, and they will go out unto the battlefield prepared to ask of another one, their form — not their life, but their form. And they will stand there ready to do battle, and in an instant of recognition they will behold the Light of that one pervading all of the battlefield.

There will abide the remembrance of the Light of oneness and the weapons will be laid down, for the belief in separation will no longer be tenable. Ones who have gone prepared to do battle, ready to thrust the sword, to pull the trigger, will experience a revelation such as occurred with my beloved brother and yours, the one known as Saul and renamed Paul: the experience on the road to Damascus where he beheld his own Light, and it was blinding. It was blinding to the eyes of the world which would see limitation. Many brothers and sisters will experience a similar revelation. It takes only an instant.

You will find ones in relationship, mates, ones who are even as they would call themselves soulmates, who have chosen to bring forth issues in order to see them healed. You will see them in conflict with each other, allowing those issues to be most visible, in a feeling of grand emotion that perhaps they have denied and carried as old baggage for lifetimes and would not deal with, experiencing a limited self-image. And they are now allowing the emotions to come up, blaming the other one for everything that has ever gone wrong. They may even arrive at the point of intending to do bodily harm, when in an instant the Light will be turned on.

You are ushering in an age of enlightenment, not because I or other masters decree that this is an age of enlightenment. Always we have known that every age contains the potential for enlightenment. But you are now decreeing that you will know enlightenment, and you are seeing points of Light. It is most revealing that one of your leaders has chosen those very words. Where did those words come from? He thinks that they came from a script writer. You have called forth those words because deep within you there is a desire to know the Light that you are, and more and more points of Light are coming on.

The days to come are days of innocence = *not knowing* separation, *not knowing* that you could be anything less than perfect. When the Child knows herself/himself to be innocent, guiltless, not separate from anyone, not separate from the Father, a grand joy wells up and must be shared. And as you are willing to uplift your remembrance, to come into an exalted state of remembrance of the Spirit that you are, you uplift all of creation — which goes beyond the specific point of focus, this realm as you know it to be, and it spreads out to the brothers, who are very real, in other galaxies. Your enlightenment reaches the farthest star and beyond.

Why? Because you are the maker of the stars. You are not separate from your creations. And as you allow yourself to abide in peace and innocence and to live the vibration of upliftment, your creations cannot help but be uplifted, transformed, mirroring back to you what you know yourself to be.

The *present* days are days of transformation and upliftment, as you remember once again the innocence of the holy Child. Be of good heart for you have chosen to usher in the new Age of Enlightenment, the remembrance of Innocence.

What Would You Ask of Me?
What Would I Ask of You?

Always, beloved one, when I am called forth by you I come as your messenger. I come as the Western Union person, with the little cap on the head, and I present to you the message you have asked for, the one which your heart is calling forth.

What would you ask of me?

Would you ask for love? Know that you are loved with an everlasting Love that is beyond human comprehension. I love you as mySelf.

Would you ask for companionship? It is yours, for indeed I am not apart from you. I walk with you on the path of Remembrance. Call upon me.

Would you ask for peace? Know that it is yours with the willingness to accept the simplicity of a deep breath. Breathe, beloved one, the Peace that is your very nature.

Would you ask for abundance of golden coins? Know that they are already yours, as the Child of a most rich Father. Know that always you will be provided for, and clothed in beauty. Consider the lilies of the field, how they grow; they toil not, neither do they worry. And yet I say unto you, that even Solomon in all his glory was not arrayed like one of these.

Would you ask for health of body? Know that as you are willing to abide in the realization of the peace of the soul, the body will reflect wholeness. Choose you always to see holiness in every situation, and the body will be whole.

Would you ask to know Who you are? Beloved Child, you have set in motion the very process which will bring you to full awareness of your divine birthright from before time began. You stand upon the threshold of entering into full awareness of all that that means.

Would you ask for power? It is yours as the Child that you are —not the power of the world, for that changes with a whim, but the power of your beingness, which is eternal and beyond the estimation of the world.

Would you ask for unlimited understanding? Indeed, beloved one, I would push all limits until you know that you are limitless. You have chosen this point of focus, known as this lifetime, because it has many mirrors for you which will show you your feeling of limitation. Not all points of focus known as dimensions of reality — with a small "r" — show you as many mirrors of limitation. There are other dimensions where you know unlimitedness. You are here in this point of focus so that you can allow the limits to be known intimately, and released as you return Home once again.

What would *I* ask of *you*? I would ask you to live your vision. I would ask you to push through the limitations and the boundaries, to experience — as you have — the challenges, and then to say, "But there is more. I know that there is more," and to live courageously from the heart. That is what I ask of you: to live the Christ life, to allow yourself to live with hope, to remember joy, to lay claim to all that the Father is, to live as unconditional Love.

For long enough has there been judgment upon this plane, of self and of others, come forth from the soil of separation. For long enough has there been a belief in separation which would say, "I am separate from my brother and sister. I am separate from my creations. And" — most of all — "I am separate from my Self, the true Self." That is where all judgment arises.

Long enough have you felt separation. Long enough have you felt judgment. Long enough have you felt sorrowful, unloved. Abide with me now in the knowing that the veil is lifting and you will know

—absolutely know — the Love that you desire. Speak with me now the words of your true self, the Self that knows, "There is no gulf of separation. I am not separate from one that I see as Jeshua ben Joseph. I am not separate from ones that I would see as the brothers and sisters. *And*, I am not separate from my Father, Who sees me as His perfect Child."

What would I ask of you? I would ask you to know your perfection. I would ask you to know yourself as I know you.

Many have asked of me, "If I am already perfect, why do I not remember it now?" Because you have chosen to know an aspect that still holds what you remember outside of a linear time process, and to say, "That will come to me." For that is what you feel. It is something that you remember deep within, and it will come to be manifest. You will claim it. But you yet believe that there is a process, something between here and there that will be traversed in time, and that the remembrance *will* happen.

You have desired to know process intimately. As the master that you are, you have thought, "I want to know process from the inside out. I want to be able to experience linear process to the point where I know my wholeness through it."

It is much the same as when you would sit at table and you would eat of a certain dish, perhaps the chocolate pudding.

And you will eat and you will eat and eat of the chocolate pudding, saying, "Bring me another. Bring me another." And you eat of the chocolate pudding until you come to the place where you say, "I know chocolate pudding intimately. I know what it tastes like. I know what it feels like. I know the texture of it. I know how it feels even to put the fingers into it and to squish it around. I know everything there is about chocolate pudding. I have been inside the chocolate pudding. I have been outside the chocolate pudding. I have been the chocolate pudding. I know chocolate pudding. I am complete with chocolate pudding."

That is what you are doing with the belief in process. You are saying that, "I will experience process until I am complete with it." And there is not judgment in that, for it brings you, beloved one, to the place of claiming your wholeness, to the place of saying, "Yes, I know chocolate pudding very well. I have been the chocolate pudding." And then you go on to something else.

You abide with a belief until you know it intimately, until you are complete with it, and even now as we speak of a belief in process, a belief in time, you are experiencing, because of your almost-completeness with the process of time, an acceleration where you know time to be yet a process, but it is not the fixed process that you and the brothers and sisters have accepted as being truth for so long. You are now seeing that time is very much relative. There is a momentum which is growing because you are saying, "I know the process of time." And you are bringing your unlimitedness, your time-less-ness into the belief in process.

For example, there are ones of your brothers and sisters, the athletes, who change their vision so that a fast ball can appear to be at a slower rate. Because you are not separate from your creations, the athlete can look upon the ball and allow his consciousness to raise to the speed of the ball — which is what happens — then the speed of the ball seemingly slows down. As one would look upon an object from the perspective of separation, there can be all kinds of "random" activity. But when one claims one's totality, non-separation, and looks upon the object in oneness, the activity that proceeds from that perspective is seen to be whole.

The Truth of your being is diametrically opposed to the voice of the world. In other words, what appears to be is only part of the whole. Allow yourself to abide with the appearance and to say, "What is the opposite of this? How can I see this anew? What is the totality of this?" And that will give you a new perspective. You are very much as what you would see as the bulldozer, pushing out the limiting boundaries of what you have thought yourself to be. You are dozing your way through the limitations — and I do not mean sleeping.

Beloved one, what would I ask of you? I would ask for the allowance of the expansion of the heart. I would ask you to live your vision, to say, "I have a vision of beauty, ideal beauty as I know in my heart, and I would see a world of beauty."

Now, to manifest a world of beauty, you will have to give up judgment. You cannot have both fault-finding and unconditional appreciation abiding together. For as you abide in judgment, you feel the constriction of the box that judgment brings with it, and you do not see beauty. But as you release the need for judgment, you will behold all and call it good. You have a statement in your Scriptures that, "God looked upon all of creation and called it good." Who is this God? It is you. Look upon all of your creations and call them good; see the beauty in them. And then the Child comes forth, the innocent Child who abides in the Kingdom of the Father.

Beloved one, I would ask you to live as the Christ that you are, to live as the master that you are. Does this mean that you must be purified, cleansed? Does it mean that you must prove yourself by earning the degrees from your universities? No. You already have your master's degree. You are already a master of manifestation, a master of process. You may put that behind your name — M.M., M.P. You are already the master. That is why you can be with the point of focus right here. It is not that you have been cast out from the company of Christhood because you were somehow deficient and you must go through all the grades again, or that you must go through punishment.

You have chosen, as the grand master that you are, to put your focus of attention upon this day and time to experience boundaries and then to allow the boundaries to be dissolved, to know your unlimited Totality. And you go about it step by step with the belief in process, claiming one aspect, then another aspect of yourself, bringing them all into integration, until you remember the whole of yourSelf, knowing not separation from any of the aspects.

Beloved one, you never look upon a separate being or a stranger. You look upon an aspect of your total

Self. So when one comes up to you, you may say in your heart to that one, "What part of me are you? Show me. Show me another part of me," and they will.

There will be ones who will come and push the buttons, and they will do it over and over and over again until you come to the place where you say, "I love that part of me that is calling out for love and understanding. I don't have to get in there and fix it. I don't have to get into me and fix me. It is okay if that part does what it does."

For as you see a tapestry, there are many colors of thread in the tapestry. And if you take one thread by itself, it may be of a color that you would judge to be drab, and you say, "That is not a color I want in my tapestry." Or there may be another thread of a color that you say, "Oh, I never have liked that color." But yet when it is woven into the whole tapestry, the thread that is seen as drab gives the contrast that allows the brighter colors to shine. The color that you have looked upon and you have said, "I do not like that color; I never have liked that color," when it is woven into the beautiful tapestry, it becomes the part that allows a richness to the other colors. That is what the threads that you are encountering are doing for you. They are allowing your color to come alive. And you agree, "Yes, Jeshua, it sure did come alive! There was a lot of feeling in that encounter/relationship." And that is true.

What would I ask of you? I would ask you to live your mastery and to call forth the other masters, who are not separate from you. I ask you to claim their wisdom, to claim their unlimited knowledge. Do not see them as above you, somehow better than you, for where does the unlimited knowledge that you ascribe to them come from? It comes from you as the Totality that you are. You are the master who has been willing to know specific point of focus right here and to be as channel, as a funnel which allows the expanded Mind to experience this point of focus.

I would ask you to live your joy beautifully, in simplicity; to find a joy in living, an exuberance; to go out into what is known as the beauty of nature and to call unto the leaf at the top of a tree, or the small bird resting in the tree, "I am you" — to call with all of your voice. Allow yourself the mastery of exuberance.

What would I ask of you? I would ask you to live each moment in great joy, to live your divine birth-right, to push out the boundaries which you have accepted as real for so long. You will find that the boundaries are very much as the cobweb: seemingly very strong, yet yielding to the touch, and then they are nothing.

Beloved one, what would you ask of me? Would you ask for love, companionship, remembrance of the one holy Child? These are yours already. Would you ask for health, power, golden coins? These are but the natural effects of your creativity as the Child of the Creator. Would you ask for peace? You are the Peace that you seek; you are the heart of Peace. As you abide in silence, aware only of the simplicity of love, you know the deep Peace of your Father. And in that Peace, which passes the understanding of the world, you remember once again that you are all that you would ask for.

What would I ask of you? Exactly what you have asked of me: to live your Christhood. For you are the Christ that I am. Everything that has been ascribed unto me is you as well. For where do those qualities come from? They come from you. From the Totality of the one Mind that knows, "I am all. I am unlimited. I am Love forever ongoing." That is Who you are. Live your Christhood. Live it in great joy. Live the Life of the One that we are. That is what I ask of you.

Ascension

Beloved Self, we will speak now of your ascension. For it is not just one Jesus of Nazareth, one Jeshua ben Joseph, who ascended or will ever ascend. No, it is the one Child, which is you, who ascends in remembrance of holiness.

There is now a time that would remember the one Source from which you have come, the One I have called Abba, our Father, and from Whom you are never separate. You have brought, in your awareness, a portion of the Light that you are to this point of expression where you identify with a certain form, a certain body, a certain personality, certain activities, profession, all of the labels you use to define self. And yet you are much more than just this point of focus, this personality.

You have allowed yourself remembrance in times of meditation, times of oneness, relaxing the boundaries of who you have thought yourself to be, and you have gone into what you would call other dimensions, other realms, and you have known yourself to be with the angels, with the masters. And then you have returned, sometimes happily, sometimes not so happily, to do the Father's work upon this plane.

What I say to you now is that you may do the Father's work in great joy. It is not something that has to be done in a seriousness, a piety, or even in a certain manner that requires lifetimes of study, great ritual, purification to make you worthy. Already you are worthy. Always you have been worthy of the Father's Love, and when the purpose of time has been fulfilled, you will remain what you have been created to be: His perfect Child.

You have been willing to bring your Light and love to this plane to work amongst the brothers and sisters, following the guidance that sometimes the mind would question. The mind would say, "Well, how can this be? It does not make sense in the world. I am sure I have been called to do something else." And yet the still small Voice within you has been most insistent, and you have finally said, "Okay, Father, I will do what I agreed to do."

The ascension is what you have agreed to do.

"Oh, my goodness. Does this mean that I have to go through trials, tribulations, judgments of the world? Stand before Pontius Pilate? Do I have to be nailed to the cross? Do I have to lay the body in a tomb and resurrect it? Well, if that's what you are talking about, Jeshua, count me out."

That is not what I am talking about. For indeed you have gone through your trials and tribulations as you are in relationship with ones in the workplace, with ones in the grouping called the family, with ones of friends, with the mate, with the hoped-for mate, even with the small ones who come as great challenge from time to time and yet allow you opportunity to open the shutters of your heart.

You have been through judgment which the brothers and sisters have given to you and you have accepted because you thought it was your duty to accept their judgment of who they thought you were and who you thought they thought you were. (The world of judgment can be a bit convoluted.) And you have been in judgment of the brothers and sisters as well, from time to time. You have known judgment, and you have found times when you have stood before Pontius Pilate and you have felt no need to answer the world's judgment, for you have stood in all of your glory and you have said silently, "I am that I am." And that was all the defense which was needed, for indeed the holy Child does not need to be defended. The holy Child is holy, whole, complete, perfect.

You have known your own crucifixion. You have come through times when you have felt you were being nailed to somebody else's cross and you have come through the crucifixion — more than one. And you have allowed the limiting belief of the world, the limiting image of who you have thought yourself to be, to be crucified, dead and buried, and you have resurrected a new image of who you are from that crucifixion. You have done this over and over.

I would not ask you to experience again the trials, the judgment, the crucifixion, the resurrection, for indeed you know well all of these. You are now in process of your own resurrection, coming out of a belief which has held you in constriction, a belief which said, "I am not worthy of the Father's Love. Perhaps in another lifetime, perhaps if I belong to the right group and I have the sanctification of that group, then perhaps I might be worthy to call upon His name. Perhaps in another lifetime I might be worthy to think about my brother, one Jesus, and to talk with him." You have come through those limiting beliefs to the place where you have said, "No, right now part of me is good enough. Part of me is the holy Child." And then you have said, "Well, where is that part?" And you have looked for it somewhere within the physical being — the heart perhaps — until you have acknowledged, in a moment of inspiration, "I am my Father's Child. I am my Father in expression. I am the Life of the Father which allows me to move, to speak, to express, to have my being." And you are in process now of your own ascension. You are the Light of the Father brought here in manifest form.

Now you are beginning to allow the Light, the radiance of the Christ, to shine forth through every cell of the body more and more freely. You are restructuring even the very DNA of the cells of the body, because you have decreed that you want to know, experience, and express more of the Christ upon this plane.

And when the holy Child, which is Who you are, decrees that It will know more of the Light that It is, then even the creation, the body, rearranges itself so that you can know the emittance of more Light. You are coming now to a time when you will see with the physical eyes the Light around everyone's body. Not just the ones who have been termed the holy ones, the mystics, the saints, as depicted in your paintings. It is a great Truth about you as well.

Now, with the radiance that you are allowing the body to show forth, with the lightness of the Spirit and the choices that you are making for lightness, does this mean that the body itself will ascend? Perhaps. Perhaps you will come to the place where you will be so light that gravity, as it has been called, will have no effect upon even the dust of our Holy Mother, the Earth that you have collected into physicality, and you will ascend the body, having changed the vibratory rate of the body itself.

But is that necessary in order to come Home? No. You can know ascension without ascending the body. It was asked of me to make a demonstration, a very dramatic demonstration for others to behold what happens when one is in a state of oneness and vibratory rate with the Light, the great ray of Light which you are. But it is not necessary to know physical ascension in order to ascend to the Father.

Indeed, you have already experienced ascension in times of great joy, times of great revelation, times when you have said, "Aha. Oh, now I understand. Now I see the Light." Of course you see the Light; it is your own Light. You experience every once in a while moments of ascension, moments which take you beyond the activities of what seems to be going on right around you, and you say, "Father, I know Your Presence even in the midst of all of the other voices calling out to me." Those are moments of ascension.

In what you see as the next twenty years of your timing, there will be a great ascension. Some of you will ascend the physical forms, and then choose to re-manifest a form, to place a focus of attention with brothers and sisters, loved ones who have not quite yet chosen to cross the threshold. You will see many of the brothers and sisters choosing for peace, for Light, for joy: some of them choosing in gentleness as a gradual process and some of them choosing because they have finally gotten tired of the pain of the world. Finally they will pause for a moment long enough to hear the Spirit of wholeness, the Holy Spirit, suggest to them another way.

In the next twenty years of your timing... Does that sound like a miracle? Yes, and it is. But miracles are quite natural. They come with the willingness of the holy Child to remember and return Home. Miracles occur naturally. When they do not occur, there is something yet held in the belief which calls out for healing.

You have agreed to bring Heaven right into this plane. Sounds like a big job. And yet, it occurs naturally as the holy Child chooses to do the work of the Father in joy and in Love, in surrender, no longer having to figure it all out, but just saying, "Yes, Father, I am here. Use me. Tell me where to go. Tell me what to say." And if there is no direct message in that moment, what should you do? You abide. You enjoy until the next moment when the Father says, "Be upon the feet and go somewhere." That is surrender. That is being willing as a little child to be led by the Spirit, to be led Home again, responding to yourSelf.

You have chosen to bring the Light and the Love of the Father into expression even with form and to temporarily set aside the remembrance of Allness so that you could know specificity. It has been called a sin; it has been called the fall from grace, and yet it has been by divine design, in order to know and to experience the Light in expression.

Now you are ascending the consciousness into the Allness which you always have been, allowing the consciousness itself to rise up, and to ascend to the Father. As you surrender into the remembrance of Allness, there is a great joy which wells up within you. For the holy Child realizes that there is nothing more that you need do: you are now the perfection which you have always been and the perfection which you will always be. There will be a grand laughter sweeping across the face of our Holy Mother, the Earth, for the holy Child will recognize, acknowledge that "I am." Period. Full stop. "I am that I am, and there is nothing more that I need do to prove my worthiness."

Then the holy Child looks around and asks, "What can I do that is of joy? Who can I go and share my love with in this moment?" And there is a great radiance which comes forth in that moment, a freedom, an ascension.

You are one who has had the courage to say, "I will come and acquiesce, for a time being, to the values of the world. Long enough so that I know the language of the world, so that I can relate to it. But I am remembering that although I am in the world, I am not of the world." As you know yourself to be beyond the dictates of the world, there is a freedom to follow the guidance of your own heart and to allow the vibration of Love to come forth in service to the brothers and sisters — not service as it would be seen as sacrifice — service because you just can't help yourself from wanting to be doing what you are doing. And if what you are doing does not bring you joy, choose anew. There is absolutely no one on this plane or any other plane who can keep you where you are if you are not happy where you are. There is no great referee who says, "You must stay thirty-five, forty, fifty years in employment with the same company so that you can earn the gold watch." What do you have when you have the gold watch? A symbol of time past.

If you are not happy where you are right now with what you are doing, choose freely. Allow the heart to be wide open and to say, "I am the gypsy upon this plane. I am the vagabond, and anywhere I choose to lay my head, that is where the Son of God can lay his head." The son of man knows no place to lay his head for he will try out one pillow and it is too hard. And he will try out another pillow and it is too soft. But the Son of God can lay his head anywhere. You are totally free.

If you feel yourself on the threshold of changes, it is because you are. There are great changes that you are calling forth because you want to know unlimitedness. You want to know oneness with the Father. You want to come Home again. Every time you choose for unlimitedness, every time you allow the heart to open, every time you abide in peace instead of judgment, you allow ascension. And when you have the courage to do that, others of the brothers and sisters are encouraged that perhaps they can look upon things in a new light, a new way. They know you. They know what you've come through. They know you've had challenges and decisions to make. And they say, "Well, if that one can choose to be happy in the midst of all that is going on, then perhaps I can look at my life differently." You have shown them a door where they did not think there was an opening. Whether they walk through that door or not is their choice, but at least you have shown them that there is an opening there, and that is a great gift.

For in time everyone will choose for ascension. Everyone will choose to come Home to the Father. And in that there is great joy, is there not? And you do not even have to make it happen. In fact, beloved one, you cannot make it happen. You have seen that often enough. You have caught a vision and would share it with someone, and you have shared with them a book that has been most uplifting for you, or you have said, "Come, you must hear this teacher. You must come to this certain church, this certain gathering. You must hear this piece of music. I know that it will transport you. You must hear the tones." And others have listened and they do not hear the tones. Others have

listened to the great music and they have been thinking what they will do on the morrow. Or they have
gone to the workshop with you and they have said,
"Well, that was interesting but tomorrow I have to get
my hair cut." And you have wondered, "Why did they
not catch the fire?" You cannot make it happen for the
brothers and sisters. But you can allow them to see
that you have caught the fire.

You allow them their path, their timing, their
choices, for indeed, there are no wrong choices. This is
very difficult to understand in the eyes of the world
that would see duality, good and evil, for when they
look upon cruelty and violence and conflict, they ask,
"Father, how can You allow that to happen?" And yet
the Father in His great Love allows all of the choices,
for every choice is the perfect catalyst for remembrance for that one.

If you were able to fix it for another one — in other
words, to get in there and change everything according to your judgment of how it should be — they
would not accept the fixing. They would have to go
back and recreate the whole mess — as you would
judge the mess to be — so that they could come
through it.

I came to understand this in my ministry. For I
looked upon Jerusalem and I wept. I wanted the
brothers and sisters to see with my eyes the vision of
radiance, of love, of ascension which I could see. I
would have "fixed it" if I could have. And I came to the
understanding that our Father, in His great Love,
does not try to fix anything, but just looks lovingly

upon His holy Child and allows the Child to play until the Child wants to come Home again.

I would do with you what is called a short meditation. I would ask you to allow the body to be comfortable.

And when you are comfortable, take a deep breath and breathe in the golden white Light that you are. Feel it coming in to the lungs, expanding the lungs. And as you exhale, see the Love that you are being exhaled to all of the brothers and sisters.

Breathe in the golden white Light and take it deep within every cell of the body. See it radiating out from the lungs, through the circulatory system, throughout all of the body to every cell. See it turning on every cell's light as it goes by — down to the fingertips, down to the toes. And exhale the Love that you are.

Breathe in the golden white Light and feel it expanding every cell of the body. Allow yourself to know the wholeness of every cell, for if there has been constriction in any part of the body, know that the Light is healing, expanding, radiating through that part of the body. You are the Father's holy Child, whole, perfect, healed.

Allow yourself now as the Light that you are to see yourself within the heart, within your own heart. Place yourself as the Light that you are within the heart: the heart as an organ and the heart chakra. Know yourself to be pulsating, radiating Light.

Feel the Light pulsating through the heart chakra. Feel the Love that expands and is expressed through the heart. See yourself as Light in the heart, expanding to encompass the whole form of the body as it would be a huge heart. For indeed you are a boundless, infinite Heart.

See the Light expanding out, filling all of the room around you. For indeed the room is full of Light.

Know your Light to blend and to be one with all of the angels, the Light beings, the guides, all of the friends in other realms, all of the loved ones you have ever known.

See that Light expanding as the One great ray of Light of the Father. *Feel* the expansion.

Now behold the one great ray of Light pulsating, activating all of the forms of the brothers and sisters, all of the forms of life process, of the plants, the flowers, the trees, the animals. Behold the Light that surrounds every created thing, and know that you are the one who has brought all of that creation into form, and you may call it good.

Breathe the Light into all creation. Feel the peace of the Father descending upon all of creation. Feel the Father's peace *as* you. Feel the Love in which He holds you.

Breathe the Love.

Breathe the Peace.

Peace.

Now, beloved one, in that state of expanded oneness you have known ascension. Know that anytime
you desire you may behold the Light of Christ. Anytime you desire, you may ascend into the consciousness of the Light. Ascension need not be something
mysterious, something beyond you, something afar off
which can only be attained by a select few. It happens
in every moment when you choose to come up higher
in the understanding and remembrance of the Totality of the one Child which you are.

Breathe the Love.

Breathe the Peace.

Peace.

On Prayer

Prayer, beloved one, is the breath of the soul, as necessary as physical breath to the body. Prayer is your connection to the Allness that you are. Prayer is the pause which allows you to remember your holiness.

In the day and time when I was recognized to be rabbi, teacher, and I spoke words which allowed others to remember their holiness, I was asked to give forth a prayer which could be learned by the ones who were following my discipline. And most often I refused, for indeed you cannot put the prayer of the soul into words, for that immediately limits it. True prayer is wordless, conceptless. It is beyond the intellectual, beyond the mind.

Others of the rabbis at that time, and the leaders of the temple, knew many prayers. And the ones who would worship in the temple were taught from an early age to learn the words of the prayers and to be able to recite them whenever the occasion came forth. But those prayers were vain utterings of words without the breath of the soul.

All of you have known lifetimes, perhaps even this lifetime, where you have learned prayers — you have learned the words — and you have even had what would be the competition, not formal, to see how fast you could run through the prayer and get to the end of it, reciting all of the words and not missing a beat.

And yet I ask of you, when that prayer was recited in such a fashion, where was the feeling of the soul? Where was the connection of remembrance with the holy Father? It was not in the prayer, was it? Therefore, I did not give forth prayers for the followers to learn, to recite in vain ritual.

But when pressed by the disciples and others to give them a form of prayer, I shared with them the prayer that I had shared with my brothers and sisters in our home, the one that you now know well.

And when I shared it with them, I gave it with the admonition that it was to be a model — a model *only*. Not to be recited as if it were magic, but as an outline for your own individual intimate prayer. For indeed prayer is the speaking of your heart to the Father.

So when I gave forth what is now known as The Lord's Prayer, it was to be an example, a framework upon which you would weave your own prayer. And I began it with "Our Father," for it was in the day and time when the father was understood to be the head of the household. Now at the point in time and understanding where you see yourself to be, it could well be "Our Mother," "Divine Creator," "Source of all." And because there is an understood intimacy, familiarity, in speaking to one's father, I chose that wording as an example. "Our Father, from Whom we have come and in whose likeness we have been created."

Our Father. Not just my Father. Our Father, universal. For every prayer, to be true, must go beyond the singular, where there would be seen to be separateness, to go to the place of acknowledging and remembering oneness of all.

"Our Father, which art in Heaven": Heaven, a realm of oneness, of holiness, of expansion beyond the specificity of individuality, of personality, of lifetime, of any mental concept; Heaven, infinite and ever-expanding Totality.

"Hallowed be Thy name": Holy, whole, perfect, complete. Holy is Thy nature. Perfection, completeness, Allness is Your essence. That is the nature of the One Who has brought you forth — and it is your nature by divine birthright.

"Thy kingdom come": The kingdom of love, unlimited, unconditional love which sees everyone as the beautiful radiant Child. "Thy kingdom come." Not as a plea, for you are not plea-bargaining with your

Father. "Thy kingdom *is* come," as "Thy will be done, in Earth as it is in Heaven." For indeed, the Kingdom is come on Earth as it is in Heaven when you remember the Father's will is only Love — pure, expansive, unconditional Love — wherever you see yourself to be.

"Give us this day our daily bread." Again, not said as a plea, but as a statement of truth. "You supply for us in every day our daily bread." Bread for the body, but more than that, the bread of understanding, the food, nourishment of the soul. "Give us our daily bread": momently, daily. Not just once and if you happen to be out in left field you have missed it. *Daily*, ongoing.

"And allow us to drink from the water of Life." That line is not recorded in your Scriptures. For one of you, in copying the ancient writings, missed that line. It was at the end of your shift and you left, and when you came back the next day you picked up at the next line.

"And allow us to drink of the water of Life": the nourishing, refreshing water as you see it nourishing the body, *and* "You allow us to drink of the knowing of Life in all of Its expression."

"Forgive us our debts, as we also have forgiven our debtors." Your Father forgives you any momentary lapse of remembrance, for He does not know lapse of remembrance. Your Father is Love. You are Love, and as you give love in forgiveness — for that is truly what forgiveness means: to give love for, in place of, limited understanding — as you forgive others what you have judged as their momentary misunderstanding, you allow yourself to abide in the space of unconditional, unlimited Love, and you know forgiveness yourself.

It is not an exchange. It is not that if you are good enough to forgive all of the ones you have judged to have made mistakes, that somehow then you will be good enough so your Father will forgive you. It is not an exchange. It is a truth: that as you are abiding in judgment, not forgiving another one, you are not knowing love yourself. But as you forgive others and extend to them the Love of the Father, you know that Love for yourself, and instantly anything that you have judged yourself to be lacking or at fault for is released, dissolved, forgotten, gone forever.

"And lead us not into temptation, but deliver us from evil." Your Father would never lead you into temptation; He does not know temptation, for that rests upon the concept of duality. A better rendering would be, "leave us not in temptation," for truly, when you turn the focus of your attention unto the Father, all duality dissolves in the Light of His Oneness, His Love, and you are delivered from the *possibility* that there might be such an idea as the concept of evil. "And You leave us not in temptation, but deliver us from the concept of separation as our awareness of Your Love envelopes us."

Whenever you pray, go first unto the place of the heart, to the place of peace, having released, at least momentarily, all of the concerns, the constrictions, the judgments of the world. Go first to the place of the heart and know the deep abiding peace that is yours for the asking.

And when you pray, pray believing that what you would ask for is already yours, for verily, it is. There is nothing that your Father would withhold from you. There is nothing that your Father *can* withhold from you. As the holy creative Child, you have brought forth all of your creations and your experiences. You select certain experiences; you try them on for size to see how they fit. And the Love which you seek is always yours. The Love which you seek can be found within the silence of the prayer of your heart.

When you tire of the pain and the hurt of the world, turn then to the place of the heart and pray the breath of the soul. Pray to the one Father Who will never, can never, abandon you; Who is there, in Truth, to supply your every need. It is yours for the asking.

Now, there are times when you would pray, in limited thinking, for specifics, and you would ask of your Father what He does not have in specifics to give you. In other words, do not pray to your Father for the vehicle, for the dwelling place, for He does not have that in specific to give to you. They are creations within your Adventure. But that which He has is yours already. That which He has is beyond the value of the world. That which He has is freely given and it is the pearl of great price.

He gives you freely of Life, of consciousness, of creativity, which is your natural birthright. Then you take the consciousness and the creativity and you apply it to the specific that you would see in your life. Pray believing that you already have, for indeed you do.

If you would know the beauty of the clouds, do not keep the head and eyes cast down. If you would know the Love of the Father, allow yourself the moments of prayer, where He is to be found. If you would know the Love of your Father, allow yourself time, your precious time, to focus upon the peace, the beauty in the heart and the beauty in manifest form rather than focusing upon what is seemingly lacking or wrong. For as you keep your focus upon what is seemingly wrong, you deny in that moment the desire of the heart.

Allow yourself the times of prayer, of true prayer. And when you do, beloved one, you will be greatly rewarded. For you are loved with an everlasting Love which the world cannot know and does not value. But you are not of the world. You are of your Father and He awaits you in the place of true prayer.

Creating the New Dream

Beloved one, you have been within the dream of the holy Child for what you would see as lifetimes, aeons of time as you measure time in this point of focus. You have dreamt a dream within a dream within a dream within a dream. Some of the dreams have been joyful ones and some of the dreams have been as the nightmares.

Now you are desirous of creating a new dream, the dream which guides the holy Child to Awakening, and this new dream will be one of a short duration because you have decreed that you are tiring of the belief in separation supported by the concept of time and of fulfillment delayed. You want to remember the totality of Self. You want to remember the Father. You want to remember Love in unlimitedness. You want to remember the power of beingness. You want to remember the power of creativity.

So for yet a little while you will be abiding within a dream, experiencing even now the stirring that heralds awakening. The Child is coming out of a deep sleep, responding to the call of daybreak, ready to greet the dawn.

The new dream comes by invitation. It comes by desire. It comes by intention. It comes by allowance, allowing it to be within your reality — small "r" — and then with the faith, the belief, the surrender which says, "Yes, it is here." With that *knowing* it comes to your experience.

Now, will a brother or a sister perhaps to the side of you, will they see it?

It will not be their experience unless they desire it with the same intensity and belief that you do, but if they share that with you, they will see Heaven as well. Anything that you want to manifest, sit with it in the heart. Desire it. Get to know it. Get to know it intimately. Visualize it. How does it look? What would it feel like? What do the energy patterns feel like? Become one with whatever you will manifest and it will manifest. That is how you manifest everything that you see in front of you. You have called it forth out of the energy that you are. You have called it forth out of your creative energy.

And ones who are in the collective consciousness of belief will experience a shared reality. In another point of focus of shared belief, reality is experienced differently. Know you that in another point of focus you would not behold bodies. You would behold Light forms, collections of energy. You would see consciousness. It is coming to your experience where you will see form, as you focus upon form, but you will also see the consciousness of that one; you will see the energy of that one, and you will see the energy fluctuate as to how joyous that one feels, how creative that one feels. You will be able to see it in vibrational energy known now as the colors, for it will be received by the physical receptors and interpreted as colors.

You will see energy patterns. You will see vibrational changes which will be received and interpreted even by the physical senses for a time, so that you may see the body and read the various areas of the body to see which ones need a bit of upliftment, balancing. At the present point of belief you can sense with the hands the energy patterns of the body. You have played with this. You have gone over a body and you have been able to sense that a certain chakra is open, and further down the body perhaps you have sensed a constriction. Already you can feel that with the sensitivity receptors in the palms of the hands. And you will come to the place where you will see energy patterns even with the physical eyes.

Creation changes, as does the energy flow. What you beheld one minute ago is no longer here. You have re-manifested, moment by moment, the reality which you experience. You feel it to be a constant because you do it in such minuscule gradations. You feel it to be a constant and yet you are recreating in every moment your reality.

That is why with a shift in perception all of your world is transformed instantly and you look upon it with new eyes. All of a sudden the pieces of the jigsaw puzzle that seemed to be at odds and ends with each other come together and you say, "Aha. I never saw that before." And all of your world is transformed in that instant.

Creating the new dream. That is what you are about. You are playing with ideas, concepts, unlimitedness that perhaps you haven't touched upon for a long, long time, and asking yourself, "What would I do if all of the restrictions of time and space and physicality and society and culture and peers and parents and relationships and employers, et cetera, if all of those restrictions were dissolved, released for a day, a week? Even two weeks, if I get lucky. What would I do? Who would I be? Where would I go? I would go beyond space and time. I would create a beautiful world. I would see the Light which activates all of the form that is upon our Holy Mother, the Earth. I would know myself to be one with all of the life processes of the trees, of the flowers, of the flowing water. I would know myself to *be* the flowing water."

You are in the midst now of playing with those unlimited ideas, and in that you allow yourself to remember Home, and to awaken. Many lifetimes you have believed that you would have to lay down the body before you would be able to know Heaven and to come Home. But then the creative Child has said, "Perhaps I do not have to lay down the body in order to know Heaven. Perhaps I can know the joy of holiness even in this point of expression, even with the form."

You are dynamic, unlimited energy. You are the great miracle that is creating the new dream because you have desired it. You bring it forth with an intensity of desire known sometimes in this world as the "C" word: Commitment. You have heard that word. You have also heard many speak against the "C" word. "Heavens, how could I be committed? I do not want a committed relationship. I do not want commitment. It would restrict me." You have heard that; you may have said that yourself from time to time.

You bring forth all of manifestation through desire, through intensity of intention, through commitment, through allowance, through setting it all in motion and then allowing, within the belief in process, allowing that process to unfold. And you surrender to the knowing that what you have desired to manifest is already manifest.

What you have envisioned, the desire of your heart, truly will manifest. It cannot help but manifest; your desire is manifest in every moment. Allow yourself to abide in the love of the heart, in the joy of the heart, in the exhilaration and the excitement of knowing unlimitedness through playing with unlimited concepts of what can be.

You are willing now to know your own power of energy, and the dream that you bring forth is one of knowing no separation. You are bringing forth a new society based upon the energy of nonseparation and the energy of Love.

For indeed, in the process of the awakening, you will play with the truth of nonseparation and you will play with inflicting upon another one your energy. And you will feel it reverberating and coming back to you multiplied. No longer will you be able to hold the belief that you can speak an unloving word or hold an unloving thought or a judgment about another with impunity.

You think now that you can look upon a brother or a sister and you can judge them, however subtly, and it will not affect you at all. You think that there is a bit of a barricade, an armoring that surrounds you, and that you can think in judgment of another one. So you will play, as the awakening unfolds, with the extension of judgment, the extension of the harsh words, the unloving thoughts — and very quickly you will choose anew. For very quickly you will see that what you send out seemingly to another one, you send out to yourself. You are the one who abides in the intensity of it.

So very quickly there will be a revision of how you choose to act and where you choose to come from. You will play a few times with pain, and then you will say, "This doesn't feel good. I will choose Love instead; I will choose mellowness." And you will see coming forth upon your plane a society which is based on Love, unconditional Love, for it will no longer be found advantageous to abide in constriction and in separation.

You will consciously know the energy that you are and the energy that others are as they activate the form. You will even come to the place of knowing that your form will walk through the form of another one's energy, or through a wall. For as you understand yourself to be energy, as you understand all of your creations to be formed from the energy that you are, you will understand that you can pass through what is seemingly a dense wall, what now is believed to be as solid, because it is in a different rate of vibration.

You will expand the energy of the creation and you will pass through it. You will also know how to levitate the form because you will be in such a state of joy, enlightenment, that you will not need the heaviness known as gravity to hold you upon the Holy Mother. Indeed, as you know yourself to be energy and you know yourself to be enlightened energy, you will levitate yourself across water.

You are bringing forth a new society, a society based on love, because you are willing to entertain a new image of who you are and who the brothers and sisters really are, and what society is for. You are willing to exchange time-worn judgments and pain for unconditional acceptance and peace. You are willing to claim a bit of joy in each day, to laugh at self from time to time, to find humor in events that other times have been most heavy.

Employment will change its nature as well. Service will be given freely because you desire to expand the heart and to express the energy that you are. The golden coins will no longer be valued as reward for service, for indeed the expanded heart will know it is its own reward. You will no longer see as necessary the exchange that goes through the gradations of separation known as a paycheck, a bank, bills, payments, etc. for the energy will be freely given and the exchange will be known and felt immediately.

You have heard that your monetary systems are going to undergo change, and indeed they will. Some of the brothers and sisters will see this as tragedy and will hold on to the old with great resistance, and when they bring changes into their experience, there will be widespread opportunity to feel that they have lost everything, that they have lost their image of who they are, the image that they have identified themselves as being. And wonderful is that loss, for the image that they have held has been limited.

Your monetary systems will undergo great change because they will no longer be seen as necessary. Now, you need not fear the change. You need not go out and bury somewhere in the ground, nor in a shoebox under your bed, the metallic substances that you hope will be useful later. Who you are is much more valuable than any metallic substance that you could secrete away somewhere for future use. In Truth, you are the one who creates the metals — precious and otherwise — and you are the one who decrees their value.

Yes, there will still be use for metallic substances, but they will be used in devising means for serving the brothers and sisters in technological development, and in structures. They will no longer be used as a means of value in exchange for energy. Love, Light energy will be seen to be of most value. And it will be seen that each one owns equally the energy. For you are that energy and there is no lack of it.

So yes, your monetary systems will be undergoing change to the place where you will no longer need the subtle separation that says, "I will do a certain activity for you in exchange for the piece of paper or the golden coins, the plastic, the I.O.U.'s." You will not need the intermediary. Every exchange will be immediate and the service will be given because it feels so good to be in the flow of energy.

The forms of education are already undergoing great change. You will behold a major shift where every small one who is birthed into physicality will be honored as the Light energy that that one is, and they will be seen as teachers. Already you have begun the process, and in time all will come to know that there is no little one upon this plane who is unwanted.

Now many of the brothers and sisters find themselves birthing — mainly the sisters — the small ones and sometimes not wanting to be encumbered with them. Part of the process of creating the new dream will be for ones such as you to honor each little one and to speak to that one in words, and in actions, that you see value in him/her. Take a little one — or more than one — under the wing. Adopt them, not with legal papers — that is not necessary — but into your heart and say, "Come be companion with me upon the journey. We will see what we can share." For the little ones have much to share.

And it will quickly come to the place where every small one is seen to be of value and is recognized to be a master walking upon this plane — which they are now, and which you are now, and which they will be in the days to come — so that your educational processes will be greatly altered, for they will be based in love and in worth, seeing the value of each point of Light which is expressing upon this plane.

There will no longer be a question of dictating the course of study that must be done. The points of Light — you and they — will be seen to be equals and there will be an honoring, acknowledging what the little one can share with you and what you can share with the small one because of where you have journeyed along your path.

You will see innovations in your health fields, where the wholeness of energy will be understood to be the foundation for health. Treatment/balancing of the energy of the body will involve knowing and monitoring not just a part of the body, not just the momentary symptom, but the energy patterns of the body as a whole.

Already you are in process of bringing forth technology that will assist you in doing this — for there is a great belief now in technology. Later it will be seen that the wisdom of one form/body is all the technology that is needed, and energy will be extended unto another one through the chakras.

Already you are bringing forth the technology to balance energy in the body through the vibrations of sound and color, and through the sound of the body itself in what is known as toning, singing, using the voice to bring about the opening and balancing in all of the chakras of the body.

There is much that you will be playing with. You will play with various substances where there is belief that the Light energy of the substances can facilitate a balancing of the form itself, where the Light energy will remind certain areas of the body of the Light that they are. That is the purpose of various nutriments and supplemental substances: to bring Light into various parts of the body, to say to the body, "Remember how it feels to be Light." You remind the cells of the Light that they are. And it is not the substance itself that is magic. It is you, your consciousness, your energy of Light that is directed through the use of that substance which allows the various parts of the body to turn their lights on again.

In the new society you are birthing with the new dream there will be many who will see your Light: the light of the body *and* the Light of your consciousness. You will find many coming unto you, seeking, and you will speak your truth in freedom. You will be planting, as you already have planted, many seeds. Those seeds in time will grow, but it is not your responsibility to make those seeds grow. In truth, you cannot make them grow for they must be nurtured in the consciousness of the one receiving them. You can only offer them.

But know that all of the words of truth you have spoken unto ones who have then walked away, those seeds will grow in time, for the holy Child is one and the holy Child desires to come Home again. Only the time — as time is seen to be — of choosing for Love, for Peace, for Home, varies. Never fail to speak words of truth to another one. For indeed they call you forth in that moment to be servant unto them, to speak, without fear, your truth. That is why you come together. That is why there is relationship, however brief. Ones are asking now to know the Truth of their being and they call you forth to share with them the Truth that you know. It is a grand gift that you give unto them, and you do not need to fear the giving of that gift.

You are birthing an energy which already has a life, a life given to it by your vision, by what you have seen to be the possibility of Heaven upon Earth. It starts first with the entertainment of the idea that there could be such a possibility. And as you play with that idea of possibility, it becomes a probability. And as you play with that probability, it becomes a reality, a reality which leads you to the remembrance of your Reality. You are creating the new dream, beloved one. Dream a dream of gentleness, of Love extended, of holiness acknowledged and remembered. Dream the dream of a new Heaven and a new Earth. Dream the dream of Love.

How To Bring About Change

Beloved one, I would share with you my joy. Will you play with me?

This evening before you lay your head upon the pillow, I would give unto you an exercise. I invite you to stretch forth the arm in front of you and to reach to the opposite shoulder and pat yourself on the back. And then, bring the other arm around in a hug of self.

Be at peace in loving the self, for as you love yourself, then you can reach out to others and love them in an expanded understanding. You have been taught that to look upon self and to nurture self is arrogant and selfish. But I say unto you that as you get to know yourself and love yourself, you uplift all of the brothers and sisters, for loving self is not selfish in the small sense; it is Self-ish, serving the one Self.

What *is* selfish is to abide in the constriction and to say, "Woe is me; how unlovable I am," for that keeps you in a place of constriction. But as you choose to live in a new energy, you uplift all of creation, near and far.

You have heard it said that you are birthing a new energy, and this is true. You are remembering fifth dimensional energy, the energy of Light experienced as Love. You are desirous of knowing expanded vibrational energy, not just to think about the concept of what love is. You have been abiding in the place for some time — many lifetimes — where you have experienced limited expression of love. You have felt human love, and you have written the love poetry which has expressed the love you knew at that time, unrequited and otherwise.

What you are now desirous of, and you are calling forth, is the awareness of unlimited unconditional love — to know what that feels like, to be accepted as the Child that you are, and to be loved as the Father loves you, not loved just because you happen to be of the right religious persuasion, of the right philosophy, or that you dress and style your hair a certain way that is acceptable, or that you have the right professional degrees and certifications, or your skin is the right color or whatever, on and on and on, but to be loved as the Child that you are, as the holy Child who has chosen, out of great courage, to express in this point of focus. You are the Child who has said, "I will come through all of the experiences known as human expression and I will remember that I am my Father's Child, totally unlimited, and I will give unto others unconditional Love, for that is what my Father does, and I will behold everyone in that Light — including myself" — for it starts with self.

You are asking to know fifth dimensional energy in most dynamic fashion. That is why you have brought forth the challenges, a great acceleration of challenges, which have come to you as experiences, some of them not particularly welcome as you would judge them, and you have asked, "Why have I called this upon myself? Why is this happening?" It is because you have said at a very deep level, "I have the courage to relive this experience and to see it anew, to heal old wounds and to see as holy that which has been judged to be unholy."

It comes because you are ready, because you know at a very deep level that you have the power — not as the world defines power, but you have the power to handle whatever comes to you and to see it in a new light. Furthermore, you have decreed, "I will have it quickly now. No longer will I work on just one aspect in one lifetime, as I see a lifetime to be. Bring it all on. I am ready for it. I want it on my stage right now."

And so, the challenges come. Little ones. Big ones. In Truth they are all the same size, but you look upon various ones and you judge, "Well, that was an easy one. And that one, oh my goodness. I don't know what to do with that one." And you sit with it and you gnaw on it like a dog would with a bone, and you chew and you chew and you chew until finally you get to the marrow of it and you find that there is some goodness in it.

You are releasing heavy burdens which have been carried throughout lifetime after lifetime, and now you are decreeing, "I wish to know lightness. How can I come into an expression of fifth dimensional Light if I carry all of these heavy burdens with me?" As you have discerned, you cannot.

When you go about with the heaviness of the world and the habitual judgments, there is not much of a feeling of Light. But as you say, "I am willing to come into a new place of understanding; I am willing to release that which does not serve the Light," then you bring upon yourself a grand experience: "I want to know Heaven upon Earth."

Now, a few years ago in your timing for one to say that, it would have been — and is still in some of your circles — a sacrilege. How could one, a worm of the dust, begin to know Heaven upon Earth? And yet what you are now decreeing is that you will bring Heaven, the experience of Heaven, the unconditional Love of the Father, to this point of focus. You will no longer believe that it is necessary to lay down the body in order to know the state of Heaven, but you can express with the physical form and still bring the energy of unconditional Love and the Light that activates form into conscious remembrance and expression. That is what you are birthing.

And when the Light is seen and experienced, there will be such a feeling of freedom that the Love will no longer be held inside, tightly rationed out because perhaps there is not enough of it to go around. But Love will be free-flowing, knowing that always there is more of it. Whenever you open yourself to the flow of Love, guess what happens? More of it is given to you, and you find yourself in the midst of a great flow, a river of Love.

Thank you, beloved one, for the Love you give to self and others. For as you have released the shutters of the heart in an ever-expanding remembrance of Love, you have found yourself first to be amidst a trickle, then a stream, then a river which quickly now flows into the vast ocean of Love, where you will behold the Christ of everyone who stands before you. And there will be such an outpouring of love that it will transform your world.

You will bring the Kingdom of Heaven into the world. It is not possible to take the world into the Kingdom, but it is most possible and necessary to bring the Kingdom of love into the world, and that is what you are about to do. You are creating change.

Now, how does one manifest change? All change begins and is created in the future. It does not come out of the remembrance of the past for that holds you in what is known as historical perspective. It holds you in the place of "this is what has been; this is the limitation of what can be. This is what mankind/womankind has always done...," et cetera. That is historical perspective, which keeps you repeating the same patterns. All change is birthed in the future by allowance — by allowing it to come into the present, by inviting it to come into the present.

Change itself is an energy, as you are, and you manifest change out of your energy known as consciousness. Any change that has ever happened has manifested because of your allowance and your willingness to invite a new perspective, a new expression to come forth. It is a wave of energy which you can ride into what you would see as the future.

You can ask yourself, "What would I like to see changed? How would I like to experience change?" And you may play with the small things and you may play with what you would call the big things. Again, in Truth they are all the same size and of the same import, but some will seem to be small — you will judge — and some will seem to be the biggies.

Allow yourself to ride the wave of energy into what you call the future, and play with imagination. Allow yourself the freedom. As we have spoken of fifth dimensional energy, unconditional love and unlimited Light, allow yourself to play with how that would feel. How would the body itself feel, knowing that it is Light? Where would the constrictions of the body go? They would be dissolved in the Light, in the fluidity of the Light. Play with how fluidity feels. Play with it in your mind, and then allow the body itself to express in what you would term a dance, a dance of Light. How would it feel to be Light, to go as the Light, free-flowing?

Allow yourself to play with how it would feel to be loved unconditionally, to know that, "I am the most wonderful expression of my Father upon this plane. He loves me with an everlasting Love, from before time began. And after the purpose of time has been fulfilled, He will still Love me. I have never sinned; I have never gone astray. I have made choices and I have played, and I am the most wonderful Being."

Allow yourself to feel that Love. Immerse yourself deeply in that Love. It is not conditioned upon anything you have ever done or will ever do. You are Love because you are His creation. Never have you gone astray. Every choice you have ever made has been for the fun of experiencing whatever would come from that choice.

You are a great master. You are your Father expressing on this plane. That is how wonderful you are. Think what that means. Allow yourself to ride that energy into the future and bring it back to the now. Ride the energy of how it feels to be the Father in expression right now, right here, in Love with everyone and every being — yourself included.

I am the Father in expression. That is what "I and the Father are one" means. "He who hath seen me hath seen the Father." I and the Father are one — not two, as I would see myself here and the Father somewhere afar off. I and the Father are one. I am that Love, and I have chosen to bring it into this experience and this expression, to give it forth as the Father gives it forth.

How can He do it without you? Verily, He cannot. And as you allow the Father's Love to be expressed through you, as you behold a loved one, a beloved pet, as your heart leaps for joy, *you* experience consciously the Father in expression. That is why I have encouraged you to love one another as I have loved you.

Now, much has been spoken about the Father's Will. Many have asked, "How do I do the Will of the Father? How do I know what His Will is for me?" I would share with you that you *are* the Will of the Father. You are the Love that is ready to be poured forth, and it is the Will of the Father for that Love to be known and shared freely with everyone, including self.

Whatever is not Love does not, in Truth, exist. But there will be seen yet, for a little while, the manifestation of what appears to be not of love. You are calling forth change because you have decreed that you are tired of experiencing what is not of love. Is this not so? You have said, "I am ready for a change. I want to get on with the good stuff." Okay, so be it.

Change is birthed in the future. Change does not come out of the past, although the satisfaction, completion comes out of the past. "I am satisfied. I am full of goodness with all that I have experienced in the past. Now I am ready for change." And change itself is an energy which comes out of the future. So you ride that energy into the future as you would ride a beautiful wave. You are an experienced surfboarder, and you ride your surfboard on the wave into the future and you bring back possibilities, which you will then play with until you know them to be probabilities. And as you abide with them as probabilities, they will become realities.

Whatever you desire to bring into manifestation, allow yourself to go to that place of possibility and to contemplate, to feel, to experience, to play with, to imagine, to know yourself to be one with it. See how it fits. Try it on for size. And as you do that, you bring it into the realm of probability.

You have been playing with possibility, contemplating new possibilities of expression upon this plane, new possibilities of what it means to live and how to live. And you are bringing those possibilities into the realm of probability as you abide with those ideas, those concepts, those feelings. And after awhile, they become your realities.

Simple? Yes. In Truth it is simple. You allow yourself the freedom of going beyond what you have known — what has been defined by historical perspective — and to bring back into the present moment to play with, something that you see to be in the future, or beyond what you now know. That is what the future is. It is seen to be somewhat beyond where this point of now is. And yet as you contemplate what you call your future, you bring it into the now. Grand mystery.

Change itself is a mystery, for as the analytical mind would want to understand the workings of change, the heart knows and allows change. Change comes with your willingness and your invitation, and that often is motivated by completion, satiation, overfulfillment of what you have experienced in the past. Then you begin to ask of the Father, and of me — I have heard you as you have prayed — for deliverance from the past, from the sorrow, from the constriction, from the burden that felt too heavy.

What you have done then, in that moment, is decree that you are willing to know change, and as you ask, it shall be given unto you. It is necessary that you come to the place of asking. It is necessary that you come to the place of willingness. It is necessary that you come to the place of clarity which says, "Okay, I am ready for something new. I am ready for something that is of love, something that feels better than what I'm experiencing right now." And then, as you ask, already it is given you.

For indeed, whatever you would ask for is yours from before time began, but you have believed a process to be necessary. As you become willing to ask for what you desire, willing to claim it, immediately, instantly it is yours.

I would do with you now a meditation, a meditation for change.

I would invite you to take a deep breath, to breathe in the golden white Light which you are, which surrounds you, which energizes you, which is you. To breathe in deeply the Light of the Spirit and to exhale the Love you are. And to come again unto that place of peace within the heart.

Breathing easily without effort, breathing the connected breath of the intake and the exhale, abiding in that sacred place of the heart, feel the peace which is yours always. Know that you can come unto this sacred place anytime, for it is your gift to yourself, this space of peace.

Know that whenever the burdens and the questions of the world are too heavy, too confusing, too insistent, you can pause and breathe deeply and return unto the place of peace that is within.

Imagine now, if you will, a filing cabinet that is yours, a filing cabinet of however many drawers you would choose. And the drawers are full of folders, file folders you call them, of beliefs —belief about everything, every aspect of experience. And into those file folders you have put what you believe about life, how it is to be experienced, how it has been in the past.

There is a file folder named relationships, and in it you have placed what you believe about relationship. There is a file folder named for every aspect of your experience, and into those file folders you have placed beliefs that have dictated to you decisions.

Allow yourself to examine one of the file folders. Allow it to come forth and to open up in front of you and to show you what your belief is about life, about who you are, about relationship, about love, about money, about God, as your Father has been called. Bring forth any belief folder and look upon the belief that is in there.

Some of the beliefs serve you well. All of them have served you in the past. Some of the beliefs you have discarded for they have been constricting and burdensome, and you have allowed them to be released, dissolved, as if written in disappearing ink. They have dissolved in the light of new understanding and have been replaced by another belief. All of the beliefs in your file folders in your filing cabinet have served you well, for they have brought you to this place.

But imagine now, if you will, another filing cabinet full of file folders on the same aspects of experience, but these file folders are listed as possibilities. When you would know a new possibility about life, bring forth the file folder labeled, "Life, Possibilities of." And look within that folder and see what you have placed there. If it is empty, so much the better. You can fill it with possibilities that are unlimited.

You are the one who writes what goes into every file folder, and if you do not like what is written in a file folder under one of the beliefs, you can take what you call the cosmic eraser and erase it, or you can apply the light of new understanding, a bit of the heat of that light to the disappearing ink and it will disappear.

The new reality you are birthing upon this plane comes out of the filing cabinet of the possibility folders. Allow yourself in your times of meditation to go into that file cabinet and to bring out various file folders of possibilities on different aspects, and to write new writings, to take all of the restrictions off. Do not be bound by the filing cabinet with the folders that say, "Beliefs, Historical," but play with the folders of possibility.

Allow yourself to know that you are the one who is manifesting the new energy that comes with possibility. You are the one who allows the possibility to come into the realm of probability and then into your reality.

Allow yourself now to feel the peace of the heart, to feel the *expansion* of possibility; to breathe new life into the desire of your heart; to imagine it, to feel it, to *be* it.

Whenever you desire to change your experience about something, return again in meditation to the peace of the heart, and call forth the file folder of the possibilities of that aspect. Abide with the possibilities and invite new possibilities to make themselves known to you. You are the unlimited creative holy Child, and all that the Father has is yours.

The space that you have just touched is always with you. It is the Kingdom that is within, the realm of infinite possibilities, infinite Peace, infinite Love. Did you have to do anything difficult to reach that space? No. The heart knows the depth of peace, and it is simplicity itself, always available to you. It is where you and I, beloved one, abide together.

There is great power and great wisdom in that place — not because you find me there, but because you find yourSelf there, your true Self. Return often to that place of peace known as the heart, for out of that space comes the future you wish to create. The world will speak to you of what has been. The world will speak to you of limitation and will say that Heaven on Earth cannot be. The world in its very short memory will say that that has never been and will never be. But the Truth of your being and the beliefs of the world are diametrically opposed.

For, what you see as possibility and bring from what you would call the future into the now is but a remembrance of what has always been, from before time began. And what you are doing now is allowing the mystery of the Truth of your being to come into this expression, not hindered by historical perspective or by what others would tell you has to be or has always been. Now you are allowing the new energy to come into the present, to activate the heart of Love.

Remember in this evening the exercise that I invited you to do: to stretch forth the arm and pat yourself on the back, and to stretch forth the other arm and hug self. For you are greatly loved of the Father, and what you call forth now is a remembrance of your holiness. You are creating change upon this plane. You are allowing possibility of radiant Light. You are ushering in the energy of Love, and Remembrance shall be your reward.

The Great Wave of Ascension

Beloved one, you have heard it said that you are ushering in a new age, and you have heard much talk about ascension. Even ones of your brothers and sisters who would use a different terminology have spoken of and are expecting the ascension, for the Family itself is calling forth a holy experience in willingness to acknowledge and experience Remembrance.

There has been much talk as to whether the bodies will ascend, will be taken up, and some of you will experience that for you will come into such a state of radiance, such a state of joy, exhilaration that you will not be able to hold the Light particles that you are upon this plane and you will ascend even what you see as the physicality, the body, into another dimension.

Already you have been playing with that. You have called forth your works of science fiction. You have seen it upon your square box and your cinema where there has been the concept, "Beam me up, Scotty." Where do you think that idea came from? From you, the holy Child who is upon the threshold, ready to ascend.

What is taking place now upon this plane is a wonderful ascension, ascending in consciousness, ascending in awareness to the realization and acknowledgement that "I and the Father are one." Those words do not apply just to one Jeshua ben Joseph, one Jesus. They apply to you. You and the Father are one; otherwise you would not be expressing. You would not be Life in its process. You would not be consciousness. You would not be creativity. You *are* the Father in expression.

Now there is a great wave which is sweeping across the face of our Holy Mother, the Earth — a harvesting, some have called it — a time when ones who are desirous and willing to ascend unto the Father are now finding themselves lifted up in consciousness.

It is a process you set in motion in what you would see as lifetimes ago when you made the decision, the choice point, to return again to the Father. And in what you have seen as recent lifetimes you have brought forth much that has been of inspiration, that has been of a new way of thinking, and you have begun to allow the Light that you bring to this plane to be increased.

The Lightness has grown upon itself exponentially and you have extended it into all areas of your experience, including the areas of technology and what you call science, your knowing —that is what your word *science* means: *knowing* — where you look outside of yourself to prove the knowing that you already know and you call it science. Now you have devised technology, ways of measuring the Light that you are, to prove to yourself the energy of Spirit, the infusion of spirit with form.

The ascension that is of most importance now is the ascension in consciousness, the ascension which says, "I will rise above all of the limiting beliefs and the limiting self-image that I have held of myself, of the brothers and sisters, and of what the world is for." And, if you will receive it, even the brothers and sisters who are not putting it into such language are also in process of ascending. Even the ones in great conflict with their brothers are in the process of ascension, where they are calling forth the very events that bring them to a place of choosing to come Home, choosing peace even in the midst of chaos, even in the midst of bombshells and gunfire — and peace is most treasured and miraculous.

There are ones even now of your brothers and sisters in the midst of gunfire who have found, much to their surprise and wonderment, that they know peace deep within them, peace which they did not believe possible, and yet all around them rages the sound of warfare. There are ones who would not have believed, moments before, that they could open the heart and love another one, and yet in one miraculous instant they have seen that other one as themselves and have extended whatever they had to share with that one, have taken that one under the wing, the arm, and have vouchsafed them.

There is much of the ascension that is in process even in what would appear to be tragedy because you have decreed that you will know your oneness. You will know your Family — not just biological family, not just the political family, not just geographical/national family, but you will know and you will experience brothers and sisters, Family, beyond the Earth dimension. You have already communion with the angels and with other dimensions, as you call them. This will continue, and will increase in occurrence and ease, for you have said, "I want to know more of my Self" — with a capital "S".

You will encounter, some of you, interaction with what you would call now your space brothers, ones who will be seen to come from another space. (Already you encounter that in your place of employment, where sometimes you say, "Where is that one coming from? He must be from another space." But that is not what I mean here.)

You have invited ones who are expressing in what you would see as other galaxies, other dimensions, to come and be part of your experience because you want to come past the habitual first reaction of fear when there is something different. Already you have had the books, the recounting of experiences which have been most fearful, stories of ones who have come and looked very different. But, after the first excitement of fear, you have said, "I want to know what is at the heart of this. I will play with this idea." You have read the books, heard the stories, seen the movie, and then you have gone to the quiet place of the heart. You have said, "Well, if I and the Father are one, and all of creation is of the Father — which it is — then I welcome more of my Self. I welcome knowing more of my expression."

So, as part of the ascension process you will see others coming to be in interaction with you. You will see them upon your computer screens writing you messages. And you will wonder, "Where did that come from?" You will have quite a great dialogue.

You will also play with the first reaction of, "This must be a higher intelligence than I am, for they seem to have come from somewhere else with greater technology than what I know, and how can they write upon my computer screen, tapping into it in a way that I don't understand?" And there will be the temptation, which you have known in many other lifetimes, to put others above you and to see them as something grander: to be feared or to be worshipped.

For indeed, the ones known as space brothers have come in a lot of other lifetimes, as you know lifetimes to be, and you have worshipped them, knowing not that they were a brother, a sister the same as you, and that you had invited them to come so that you could get past the idea that there would be the gradation, the levels of worth and wisdom.

You call this forth because you want to know ascension. You want to ascend out of the limiting belief of who you have thought yourself to be and what you have thought life *could* be. You are playing in your cinema with ideas that go beyond what you know in your everyday experience and you get excited about these ideas. There have been great servants of the Father who have brought forth stories to allow the brothers and sisters to play with new ideas in a non-threatening way. It is aiding the ascension.

For as you allow yourself to abide with what would seem to be a strange idea, after awhile it is not quite so strange and you begin to see more aspects of it in another light, more understanding, more familiarity. And many of you will be experiencing encounters, if you so desire. After the first surprise, allow yourself to breathe — yes, to breathe, to come to that place of centeredness which allows you the choice, and then to say, "I will step back from this drama for half a second, at least, and I will behold what is going on." Play with it.

Will the space brothers come to save some of you because you are more worthy than some of the other brothers and sisters? No. No one can save you — not even I — for you do not need saving. The holy Child is as he/she has been from before time, perfect and whole, but, with divine purpose, you have decreed that you will know experience and expression within the drama of the Adventure. For yet a little while you will play.

Will the space brothers come to destroy the Holy Mother? No, this cannot be. Do they come because they are interested to know life upon this plane? Yes. They come by invitation, your invitation as part of the process of ascension, and they come because there is a reunion of all of the Children — as they see themselves to be individuated — of the Father.

So they come to know what you experience, to experience with you and through you, life upon our Holy Mother, the Earth. You will find creative ways to interact with them, ways perhaps not of the direct communication of the words: it will be heart to heart and mind to mind. Already you are moving into knowing mind communication with what you call ESP, communication which goes on beyond the sense of the body. So you will be creative; you will find a way to meet, to commune, to know oneness even though outward appearances look different. And they will feel a welcome. For indeed, they also deal with some of the habitual fear. Some of them will come wondering what sort of welcome or non-welcome they will receive. They deal with their own images and expectations. But as they feel a welcome from you, heart to heart, then the communication can happen.

It is not by accident that one of your recent books about an encounter of this kind was labeled "Communion." The message that was relayed in the book had a basis in fear, but the title itself conveyed much. That is part of the wave of ascension. The brothers/sisters come by your invitation now because you are desirous of knowing more of the totality of Self and how It expresses.

Ascension need not be something and is not something that is going to be a great event that happens just once, is heralded by your newspapers and on your T.V., and has all of the choirs of angels singing. Ascension happens in every moment you choose to see in the light of peace and love. Every time you say to yourself, "I can see this differently," and you bring the Light of your own inner wisdom to shine upon whatever is happening, it is part of the wave of ascension.

Some of you will experience ascending the body into what you would see as another dimension and then you will come back again. Some of you have already experienced ascending into the Spirit and going somewhere else, as you would call it, although there is no where else to go, and then you have come back to this point of focus.

You have done what you call the cosmic travel and then, instantly, as you have realized that perhaps you were traveling somewhere, you have found yourself back in this point of focus.

But in the moment that you allowed yourself to release the boundaries of what you thought reality to be, in that moment you have ascended. And as you allow yourself consecutive moments of conscious oneness and you have loosed the boundaries of self, you will find yourself abiding in ascension. You will find yourself to be unlimited. You will find yourself to be the joy of the holy Child of our Father, and you will know that all is possible to you — because you *are* all.

Will you know ascension with the release of the body? This has been a religious belief, a philosophy, a hope. No, not necessarily. You have tried that. You have said, "I want out." And by various methods you have deceased the body. You have laid it down, thinking that in a moment there would be Heaven, ascension, conscious oneness, bliss, and you have found, "Uh oh, I still have my fears." And you have experienced more of a nightmare in those times because you did not then have the buffer of the process of time before there was instantaneous manifestation of those fears. What you give to yourself in this point of focus, with the belief in time, is a buffer where you can play with an idea, you can play with a fear, the "what if?" You can feel all of the dimensions and constrictions of it, and then have the opportunity for choice before you are right in the middle of the immediate effect of that choice.

So you have laid down the body in other lifetimes, thinking that you could ascend to a blessed relief from the sorrow of the world, and you have found yourself still with the blinders on — good descriptive word — the blinders that kept you in the same set of beliefs, the same consciousness, and instead of experiencing Heaven, you have experienced the old fears.

You have had your religious beliefs, philosophies, which have taught that after you lay down the body you will go, if you have not been deemed good enough, unto a place called hell. And many of you have experienced that. You have bought the belief, bought it dearly, and you have experienced hell. But it does not last forever, and you made choice then to say, "I want to have another take on this. There must be another way to experience Life" — as there is.

Now you are very much upon the threshold of experiencing ascension out of the constriction of limited belief, limited self-image. Blessed are you, for it is a grand time to be experiencing this plane. Even for the ones who know conflict and are in the midst of gunfire, even for them it is a grand time because they are calling forth exactly what they have deemed necessary to allow them to awaken. And in a moment, in an instant, the ascension happens.

You will play with ideas of the mind, intellectual concepts — they are fun to play with — and then as you pause for a certain breath in the midst of the intellectual conquest, the heart speaks true to you and says, "Yes, I know this. I know this at a very deep level." You *do* know it, for you are the very one who has called forth the information that you are contemplating. That is how powerful and wonderful you are.

You have written the books that you study, the books that you find inspiration in. You have written the ancient classics, and now you come in what you would see to be another lifetime, rediscover them and say, "Wow, this stuff is really great." Of course it is great, because it is part of your process of ascension.

The holy Child is ascending out of the narrow identification with the density of matter to know the Spirit which activates the matter. You are doing this in all areas of experience. You, and the brothers and sisters, have chosen areas of expertise, areas of service, areas where you can bring expanded understanding, and you add to the upliftment of the consciousness of the whole. Every day in what you see as your technological fields you call forth the advancements that bring the world as you understand it to be —geographical distance, philosophical difference —

closer and closer together. You have spoken of how the world is shrinking. You have said, "It is a small world." You are experiencing the perceived decrease in distance of separation because you are wanting to know that you are one. Whether you sit right here or across the face of our Holy Mother, the Earth, you are still the one who is expressing and experiencing.

So you now have the technology where you can speak with one on your videophone halfway around the face of our Holy Mother, the Earth, or you can type in one of your messages and it is sent through your electronic mail instantaneously.

Why? Because you want to know that you are beyond time. You want to have it now. You want to be it now. So in every day of your timing you bring forth more creativity to prove, yet from the outside as it would look to be, that you are bonded one to another in mind, and heart.

Even the physical body you transport much more quickly than you used to believe possible. At the turn of your previous century it took many, many of your days to traverse the face of your country. Now you can do it in a few hours, as you take the physical form and move it through the clouds, allowing your consciousness to expand right in front of you.

For indeed, you manifest your body, the form, in every moment. In every moment you call it forth in newness. That is why there can be instantaneous healing: you manifest the form new in every moment, and the reality that you experience — with the small "r" — is your consciousness, prescribed by your beliefs.

And in a few years of your timing, you will no longer see it necessary to place the form upon or within another object, vehicle, to transport it to another place. You will know the consciousness that you are, that is just beyond the nose, to be unlimited and you will transport yourself to another place just by thought, allowed by belief, and by the activation of the vibration of your energy in a way that you would see, from this point of focus, to be different than what you do now.

In that time it will seem most natural, and no, you will not bump into each other as you go. You will not have to have your air traffic controllers — or your Spirit traffic controllers. Instantly you will think of where you want to be. You will visualize it. You will activate the vibration of energy that you are and you will be there.

Now, as I speak those words, there is a resonance somewhere within you which says, "Yes, that could be possible." Know you that as you have had the resonance to say, "Okay, I can imagine that," you will bring it forth. For the belief which supports that reality is just beyond the nose — what you believe to be the boundary of reality — and very soon you will walk into it. You will accept it as the truth of your being. Your belief will be, "Yes, I can do that." For indeed you can.

Already you have found yourself to be experiencing another dimension, another space, as you have been in meditation and you have felt yourself transported, uplifted into communion with another one somewhere else, but you have said, "Well, that is just my imagination. It didn't really happen because I know the form was right here." But are you sure? In that moment of being with the other one in what you thought was just your imagination, you were not focusing upon the form. Where was the form?

You are unlimited. Whatever you wish to call forth to facilitate the ascension you will call forth, for you have decreed that you will come Home. You will know oneness with the Father — not just as a great idea that someone is rumored to have done long ago. "Well, there's one Jeshua, who did great things two thousand years ago because he was the Son of God, but he's way above me." No.

I chose to know the energy of Light and Love. I chose to study with others who allowed me to remember what they knew. "Well, he had the advantage of studying with masters." What are you doing right now? What do you do in every moment when you call forth the books of inspiration? You study with the masters.

I chose to know my unlimitedness. I chose to allow the brothers and sisters to see that there is life always and that the form can be laid down, dead and buried, put away in a cave, and yet resurrected. For always you are Life. You are the energy of the Spirit of Life that brings the form into activation.

I had practiced certain understandings of the vibration of energy. I had not yet practiced the laying down of the body to the point of deceasement of the body and then resurrecting it, but I knew the principle. I had not had occasion until the time of the crucifixion to come through that experience. But I knew it to be possible — as now you know it to be possible — and I had studied with other ones who knew how to ascend their body, to materialize it in another place, another time.

I knew how it felt to raise the vibration of the body in oneness with the Father. I knew how it felt to walk upon water. I knew how it felt to walk through what was seemingly the solid form of a wall, and I disappeared from the visible sight of others when it was expedient.

The ascension which was witnessed in my day and time occurred because I knew myself to be one with the Father. I knew myself to be one with unlimited Love. I knew myself to be Light, and I took myself lightly, which is what you are learning to do. I knew the joy which allows one to rise up over all of the limitation of appearances. That is how you ascend: it is to know the joy, the exhilaration of joy — not just happy. Happy is great, but joy is a certain vibrational frequency and it allows you to ascend even the particles of the body.

As you choose for peace — seemingly a small choice, but sometimes a very difficult choice, for there is part of you that says, "No, I'm not ready to give that up yet. I am going to stay right in there with this thing. I'm not going to choose for peace yet. I know that that's an option and I'll get around to it. But right now I'm going to really harbor that feeling."

Okay. But each time you choose for peace, it allows you to come closer to knowing the joy which allows then the ascension in consciousness and even in physical experience.

Each time you choose for Love, you are affirming that you are more than just the event that is happening around you. Each time you choose for Love, you are allowing communion with the oneness you are, for in the moment of great Love, you do not see bodies, nor the separation that bodies would speak of. You know only a great upliftment of feeling which is expansive.

As you abide in the place of Love, the place of oneness, the place which does not recognize self — with a small "s" — or any differences of self, then you allow your frequency to be uplifted, ascended. And in a moment of great love, when you know no boundaries, you will hear the choirs of angels singing. Are they apart from you? No. They are your own vibration of Love come into your awareness. And every time you choose for peace, the angels sing, for it means that the holy Child is that much nearer to the ascension into conscious oneness. As you listen for the angels, beloved one, they do sing. There is quite a choir.

The world you find yourself experiencing is very similar to what you would see and identify in your history as the time when I walked the face of our Holy Mother, the Earth. For indeed the civilization, the lack of love between brother and brother, and the presence of love between brother and brother, quite literally and figuratively, was much the same as it is now. There was the love of sister to sister and the lack thereof, and the confusion and the sorrow was very much the same as what you experience now in your world.

There were conflicts, wars, savagery, perceived separation from a brother or sister where ones felt they could impose all manner of motivation upon others to lay down the body, coming from the belief that what they would inflict upon another one would not come and sit upon their own doorstep. And in time it came full circle and they found it was right there, at their doorstep. The world in my day and time was not vastly different from what you experience now.

This is a time of ascension, but not the ascension of one Jesus, the Christ, one Jeshua ben Joseph — not the ascension of just one holy Son of our Father. Now it is the ascension of you in remembrance of the One that we are. Choose for peace even in the midst of conflict, confusion, criticism, even amidst the honking of the horn of your vehicles. Choose for peace. Choose for love, unlimited Love. Allow the heart to open, and in that moment listen for the choir of angels, for it will transport you into the space of great joy, allowing you to know your ascension.

This is a time of ascension, and you are calling it forth. Ascend unto Me, beloved one.

The Dimensions of Ascension

Beloved Child, you are now upon the threshold of realizing the power of beingness, the power of ascension which goes beyond the reality you have claimed to be reality. I would speak with you now about the dimensions of ascension, of going beyond reality. What you see before you is reality, is it not? It is a certain reality. The book, there is a certain reality to it. The dwelling place; the furniture that supports the body — this is reality, is it not?

It is reality, yes, but not all of Reality. It is an accepted reality, for you have said that collectively, with your brothers and sisters, you will agree upon the sandbox that you will play within. And you have agreed collectively that there will be certain parameters, a certain paradigm of belief as to what this reality is. You have agreed momentarily that you will not walk through another object and yet it is quite possible to change the energy and to walk through what you would see to be dense form: a wall, a piece of furniture.

You are upon the threshold of remembering that you have done this before, for indeed you would not be even playing with the idea that this could be if there were not, deep within your memory, the knowing that you have already done this.

For in the beginning of knowing physical creation, when we thought to bring forth physical creation — one of the dimensions of ascension — we knew ourselves to be Light and we knew that whatever we created we brought forth out of Light into physicality as light coalesced.

Now, the essence of you, the Isness of you, is beyond light itself. Light is within the physical realm, and the Isness, the Beingness of the holy Child that is from before time began, is of the essence that is beyond light, beyond vibration, beyond anything that you would know as physical.

But when we as the holy Child thought to bring forth physical creation, we decreed that in the physical realm we are light and that all manifest form comes from the coalescence, bringing together, of light energy into certain vibration, a certain density of vibration. And we brought forth beautiful creations, creations of lightwaves which we swam amongst, much as you would see the living forms in your oceans. For we brought together a knowing of Light, and we were amidst and amongst the creations. And we knew easily how to go through the light which was coalesced into a creative form.

So when we speak in this day and time of being able to walk through the density of form, you know it well. There is a belief in this point of time which says, "That is something that happened aeons of time ago, almost beyond memory, or perhaps I will know it in a far off, distant future." And yet it is not beyond your imagination, is it?

You are bringing forth the most magical times. Already you are in process of playing with unlimitedness. You bring forth your science fiction, saying, "This is a future time. This is something that perhaps the brothers and sisters who will be a bit more wise than I will do. They will have the space travel and they will know how to do everything." And you throw open wide the shutters of the mind and you play with unlimited possibilities. And what happens when you do that?

There is a certain excitement, a certain feeling of exhilaration. That is why you enjoy the science fiction. That is why you enjoy going beyond what is known in this point of time, beyond the collective agreement. The feeling of expanded possibilities is a dimension of ascension for it allows you to escape momentarily what you have felt the restrictions of this reality to be.

Many times during the course of a day you have opportunity to know a dimension of ascension. As you allow yourself to abide in the quiet place of the heart, having stilled the mind and body with the gift of a conscious breath, calling to awareness the peace that is you, you touch a powerful dimension of ascension. That is a key, if you will, to the remembrance of ascension.

For indeed ascension is something you have already done. Otherwise, I would be speaking words that would have no relatedness. But ascension is something you have already done, and it is something that you are now coming to claim again as reality.

Every time you choose to abide in the heart, in the place of stillness, the place of peace, the place of love of self and of others, you choose for ascension. You choose for a new reality. You go beyond the reality you have claimed up to that moment. I am asking you now in this moment to choose to go beyond reality as you have known it.

Now, what I ask you to do is not difficult. For indeed I will share with you that you would not be communing with me in this manner if you had not already chosen. That is how far along your path, as you would see a path to be, that you are. You have already made choice to go beyond a reality that has been limited, constricting, a reality that has been confusing, sorrowful at times. You have already made choice.

I have a gift that I will share with you in this moment, and yet I cannot give to you anything that you do not already have. But I have a gift that I will share with you in this moment and it is the gift of the good news that the ascension will not be denied. It cannot be denied.

Now, you may see yourself from time to time delaying a bit, but you will not stop your own ascension. The process you have set in motion, the process of ascension will not be halted. Not by you and not even by the brothers and sisters who find themselves now in a place of great intense completion of issues.

For you are witnessing a time of polarity, a time when there are ones who are choosing to abide in the heart of love and to believe that the glass is half full — in Truth, completely full — instead of half empty, and you are finding others who are saying, "No, for awhile yet I will believe that the glass is half empty and I will be in lack, in sorrow, in confusion. I will be right in it because I want to know it completely and be finished with it."

And you, as the lover that you are, have tried to show them that it could be otherwise. But they have said, "No. I must know completion. I must do it myself all the way until the last drop is drunk." And you have said, "But it is not necessary. I have already drunk that cup for you. You don't have to do that." And they say, "Yes, I do. I have to know it for myself."

The same has been said of me: that because I suffered upon the cross, because I was crucified, dead and buried and rose again to ascend to the right hand of the Father, therefore I have done it for all of us.

And this is true. I have drunk of that cup. I did ask my Father if perhaps it could be passed beyond me, that I would not have to drink of the cup. But it was necessary to drink of that cup, and so I drank of it and I emptied the cup.

But what I have done is what you are doing — sometimes literally, for indeed you have known crucifixion, literal and figurative. And you have come to the place of completion. You have said, "I want to know now, where is the good stuff? I will drink of the good stuff." And your Father says, "Here it is. It has been in the cupboard all along. It has been waiting for you. Drink now of the good stuff." Drink now of the ascension and the dimensions of ascension which take you beyond the reality that has been agreed upon, the reality that says, "Life must be a struggle." You know that reality well; you have played that reality many lifetimes and in this lifetime. You know that reality from the inside out.

Now you are ready to know the added dimension of ascension. Now you are ready to go beyond. That is why you call forth the books which speak to your heart. That is why you call forth the teachers and the workshops, the friends who have revelations to share with you.

You are ready to claim the next dimension of ascension which defines a new reality.

So you will be making many changes.

The new reality which goes beyond the collective reality that has been known so well, that new reality is yet just beyond the fingertips. That is how close it is to you, and you can almost grasp it. And as you allow yourself to play with dimensions which go beyond this reality, you will get your fingertips right onto that new reality. You are the creator of that new reality. No one else is going to do it for you. Not that I would not be willing, but I cannot do it for you. You are the creator of that new reality.

As you allow yourself to go into a dimension which is beyond what is known, even at this point of belief, as reality, you allow yourself to expand into the "what if's" — "What if there is life on another planet? What if all of the universes are made of light and there is more light out there than I have thought possible? What if I can know travel with the body and with the mind to the farthest universes? What if I can speak with my brothers in space? What if I can speak with my sisters in the Pleiades?" As you play with those "what if's," you move yourself into a new dimension beyond previous reality, into a dimension of ascension. Never think that when you allow yourself to daydream, when you allow yourself to abide in meditation in what seems to be a far place, that you are being trivial or frivolous, for what you do in those moments has great import for this reality.

You have had moments in meditation when you have traveled more space than could ever be measured and you have interacted with brothers and sisters in a realm that knows no translation into this reality, as yet. And you have come back from that meditative place and you have felt exalted; you have felt a newness of energy, renewed, cleansed, revitalized, and you have wanted to share it with a loved one. You have said, "I feel so good. I've been somewhere, but I can't explain it. I just know it feels..," and you have tried to put it into words and yet you knew that the words did not quite convey, could not capture the expansiveness of that feeling.

As yet, for a little time, there is not the relevancy in this point of reality which will allow the description. But as you have the courage to go beyond reality and to play with dimensions which are beyond, you push out the boundaries and you begin to bring a new language into this reality that allows for ascension, the place of great joy.

For the place of ascension *is* one of great joy, of great expansion, of unlimitedness. It is the space where you know beyond any doubt that you are your Father's Child in whom He is well pleased. You know that you are loved with an everlasting Love that knows no conditions, and that no matter what you would do or say or think, His love for you will never be diminished. There will never be a reprimand; there will never be a judgment that you are less than perfect. It will always be, "Beloved Child, you are My Love."

You never have to rehearse what you are going to say. You can be most spontaneous, coming from the heart of Love, for you are the most beautiful, precious Child of our Father and you have been having a grand adventure.

And the ascension, for yet a little while, is part of the Adventure — until you know yourself to be the Adventure Itself. You are the creator of the Adventure, living the Adventure, creating the script of the

Adventure, playing the hero, the heroine, the villain and all of the supporting roles. And then, because you desired it, you did some improv and you changed the script. "Now I will have a new adventure."

You *are* the Adventure that goes beyond reality. You are the one who has drawn up the rules which define what reality is, and even now you are in process of changing those rules. You are doing a rewrite even as we communicate in this manner. For if you will receive it, when you lay aside the book, you will know a measure of ascension. You will have shifted the image and perception of the reality you accepted when you opened the book.

Beloved one, in the place of reality where you sit now you would say, "The miracle is the ascension." I would suggest unto you that the miracle is the manifestation of form that you do so well in every moment. Think upon that for awhile.

Now as we have spoken earlier, the true essence of you goes beyond anything physical; it goes beyond light itself, for light is still speaking in physical terms. And when you come to the creation of manifest form, you are speaking of bringing the energy of Thought into the physical realm, and for agreement, within this point of reality, we have chosen to call it light.

Now, if we were having this discussion in another realm or on another body of mass known as a far galaxy that knew other expression of physicality, we might not be speaking of light as an aspect of manifestation. It would be Thought and Thought come forth into manifestation in what would be defined within that reality as physicalness. But that physicalness could be and is vastly different from what you know as physicality.

What we are speaking of now is another dimension of ascension, for in this last moment when you allowed yourself to go into a reality beyond this reality, you knew ascension beyond this reality.

You are upon the threshold of a grand time. There are energies which you are going to feel pushing you. Already you have felt that. You have felt an unsettling, an unsettling to the ego that would want to know what is around the next corner: "Where am I going to be a year from now?"

Well, I will tell you, beloved one, you are going to be in the Kingdom of the Father where you have always been, but you are going to know it more, for the process of ascension you have set in motion will not be denied.

Go forth with great courage. Do not allow the reality of old to hold you, for indeed it cannot. Claim the new reality. In my Father's house are many mansions — not just cubicles, but mansions — great realms of expression and experience. And when you know completion with one realm, you know yourself to be the ascended holy Child who is the Adventure, and then you set out on the next adventure. With remembrance? Yes. Or, if you choose to be the servant of the Father once again as you are now, you take upon yourself the cloak of forgetfulness for a time to assume a language and a reality that others are playing with. For that is what you have done even in this reality: you have assumed a cloak of forgetfulness momentarily so that you could play within this sandbox.

Enjoy the last remaining years of the physicality where there is yet the collective reality which agrees that there is a density and a limitation. Enjoy them. Life does not require a struggle. Know that you are moving into the next dimension of the ascension even as we speak, for each time that you choose to be in the place of expanded reality, you choose for ascension and you know the next dimension. So enjoy the time interval you have agreed that you will share with the reality of the brothers and sisters, but choose often to go beyond reality into the remembrance of your one Reality.

Enjoy each new dimension of ascension, for as there is belief in process, so will there be belief in dimensions. In Truth, the ascension occurs in the twinkling of an eye and has already been completed, but within this sandbox there is yet the belief that it is to come. Honor each new revelation. Savor the feeling of unlimitedness that comes with expanded reality. Live in awareness. Honor the holy Self that *is* the Ascension.

The End Times

Beloved one, I would speak with you now about what have been called the latter days, the end times. To use such labeling has a bit of foreboding to it, does it not: the end times? For the end times have been spoken of as a time of doom, a time of judgment.

I would suggest unto you, if you will receive it, that the day of judgment is past. For long enough has the holy Child lived in judgment of self and others; you have known well the day of judgment. Now you are calling forth a new paradigm in the understanding of ascension. Whenever you are in judgment of self or others, you are still accepting the habitual historical perspective that one could be less than perfect, less than holy, and that there would still be something that needed to be perfected.

Allow the day of judgment to be past, completed. It is not something that you would see as a future time, for indeed you have lived with the day of judgment many days in this lifetime and all of the days of other lifetimes. Allow yourself now to choose for ascension.

The end times. For some they will be seen as a time of judgment, a time of doom, for they hold yet the image of themselves as unworthy, feeling that there must be struggle, that there must be payment in order to know the Love of the Father. There are some who will come Home to the Father through much of hardship, much of sorrow and much of conflict because that is how they have decreed they will be purified and worthy.

The Father has not decreed that they must go through the challenges, for the Father sees His Child as perfect and loveable from before time began: loveable because you are the creation of Love. You are the love that you would seek.

Now we may speak of the end times as a time of joy. It is a time of ending limited belief about self and others, limited understanding of what the world is for. The world is not a place where you have to learn lessons, where you have to come through sorrow and suffering. In truth you have brought forth the world as your playground, to play in joy, but as you would see even now the small ones as they play in the sandbox together, they do not always play in joy, do they? And neither have you.

That is not said in judgment. You have chosen to experience both sides of the coin. Having accepted the collective belief in duality, which is a shared belief upon this plane, the belief that there is good and that there is evil, that there is the opposing force and that there are all gradations of value between good and evil, you have said that you will experience both sides of the coin.

Now in truth, the coin is one. It is whole. But there is yet held a belief that there are the two sides. So there will be many of the brothers and sisters who look upon the end times with fear. For they fear that they will be judged and found wanting, and they are hoping that there will be a merciful savior who will come down from the clouds somehow and take them to the Father.

In Truth, there *will* be a merciful savior who will take you to the Father, but it is not I as a separate being. I cannot save you. In Truth you do not even need saving. You are holy already and perfect from before we brought forth the concept of time. But the savior will be the enlightenment of you. It may seem to be an embodiment, perhaps, of the light that you are and it will come from a higher perspective so that it could be seen to come from the clouds somewhere. It is symbolic.

You are your own savior, and you are in process of ascending to the Father. The end times are times of great joy. Allow yourself to claim happiness, upliftment, to live the ascension and to spread that gospel. For you will meet many of the brothers and sisters who are ready to speak of judgment day and to ask you if you are saved.

And you will speak unto these ones who ask of you if you are saved, "Yes," for indeed you are saved. And, "Do you accept Jesus as your personal savior?" And you may say, "Yes," to that as well, for I am not separate from you; I am very personal. As you are your own savior, you may claim me as your savior, knowing that we are one.

For when I said, "Lo, I am with you always, even unto the end of the world," it was not a promise, but a statement of a great Truth, for I am one with you as the holy Child of our Father. It cannot be otherwise. And I am with you always and forever, precisely unto the end of the world which believes in separation when you will know —truly know — that we are one: I and the Father are one, as you and the Father are one.

That is what I meant by, "even unto the end of the world." For at the end of the world belief in separation — upon which threshold you now stand — there will be the grand awakening in the recognition of holiness, the wholeness of One. For if you are Life — and I assure you that you are — you are the energy of the Father come into expression, and as you allow yourself to claim the expansion that is truly you, known as Love, you come Home in great joy. The end times are upon you and they are times of joy — as you so choose.

Now, there have been many prophecies about the end times. You have heard prophecies that ones will come in my name and that you must be wary. I would suggest unto you that all those who come in my name are your servant. For indeed you have called them forth. And you have heard brothers and sisters saying that perhaps one particular teacher is better than another one. You have seen repeatedly the evidence of the belief in separation where ones will say, in a variety of subtle — or not so subtle — ways, "My teacher is better than your teacher," and will foster feelings of competition. All teachers come because you call them forth. All teachers have a gift to share with you. That is why you have asked them to be within your consciousness, within your awareness of life experience. All teachers have gifts.

Allow yourself to feel at peace with everyone who comes to share with you their gift. Take from what they share what feels in alignment with your heart, and allow the rest of it to be given to someone else. Do not abide in conflict or in judgment, for that keeps you in a place of constriction. It does not allow you to see the true value of their gift.

But if what they speak is not the truth of your heart, then you may walk on. For indeed you will find others who will speak the truth of your heart, and the ones who have spoken what is not at your place of resonance have also given you a great gift because they have allowed you to call forth the clarity of your own heart to assess what your truth is. That is why you have asked them to be with you. It is much as you would ask ones to set forth the great smorgasbord for you. It does not mean that you are going to eat of everything, including the brussels sprouts and the spinach — or you may — but it has been offered for your choice.

Be at peace with all of your teachers, for indeed, by their fruits you will know them. For if what they give as a gift allows peace in the heart, unconditional love and acknowledgment of each one as the holy Child, then you will know where their heart is.

If they bring forth fear, judgment of others, the separation of competition, then you will want to assess that and see if that is your truth. And if it is your truth, abide with it.

In other words, allow everyone their path. Allow everyone their journey, for indeed everyone is on the journey Home.

But choose you well whom you will serve — not because your Father is going to judge you and to send you off to a place of great fires, but because you are the one who has to live with the experience of your choice. It is as simple as that. You see, no great complexity.

You have decreed that these are end times because you desire now to know joy, to know love, to know the Father and to come Home in the full realization even while activating the body, even while having experience upon this plane.

The end times are times of great celebration, times as you have decreed, perhaps, of the exams, because you have asked of yourself to know, "How am I doing?" So you have set yourself in this lifetime some of the tests, you will call them, some of the mile markers, in order to know, "How am I doing with this?" In any moment you can ask of yourself and receive information as to how you are doing.

For if you feel at peace with self, if you feel in love with the one who stands before you, if you feel in love with life, if you feel expanded even to the place of angelic realm, then you are knowing ascension. If you feel in constriction, in doubt, in worry, in judgment of self, that is okay, for as you become aware of where you are abiding, then you have opportunity to change, to choose anew.

Belief has brought forth all that you experience. Belief now is expanding into the possibility that you can know ascension, that you can know the magic without having to suffer and to make yourself more worthy. Belief now in this age is allowing the holy Child to play with unlimited concepts and to say that, "I know I live and move and have my being in more realms than just this one." And you bring forth the writings and the videos of imagination.

You are bringing forth a great acceleration of technology that serves you, that allows the one Mind to be in communication with Itself no matter how far removed you would see the other part of It to be. You are bringing forth the technology that will measure the energy of Spirit. Already you can do that. You can put it upon the photographic plate and have a picture of the energy.

You are bringing forth technology to know healing of the body, to be able to bring forth healing in ways that are instant. Now, I am speaking here of technology, but I am also speaking of the ancient methods where you have known that there does not need to be utilization of mechanical equipment, as you call it, in order to effect healing. You are bringing forth remembrance now that you are the energy and as you would facilitate for another their remembrance of energy, instantly there is wholeness.

For indeed time is a construct in this point of belief, and, as you are willing to play with the possibility that time does not have to be a long process, you bring forth instantaneous healing —measured even within the concept of time as being instant, for that is still within the belief system based upon concept of time.

The ascension which you will be bringing forth is the acceleration, still within time, of the particles of light which will be seen to merge into a great ray of light, and you will ascend. The form, the body, can then be remanifest as you desire.

Now, as I speak these words, there is a place of relevancy within you. In other words, you say, "Yes, I can imagine that. I don't know how to do it, but I can imagine it. I know it as a possibility." If you will receive it, all that you can imagine, all that you can accept as possibility, is already reality. You have yet what you would call a delay process which holds it in the future. But it is a reality that you know. Otherwise, I would be speaking words which would be sounds with no meaning. But there is meaning even though at this point in time, as you see time to be, you see ascension and remanifestation of the body as a future possibility.

Now, after my ascension, which is recorded in your holy Scriptures, I ascended unto the right hand of our Father. For indeed I never left, as you have never left, the right hand, the left hand, the lap of our Father. Did I remanifest my body and come back again to what you would see as this plane? Yes. That is not recorded in the usual Scriptures. You have writings which speak about the rest of that lifetime — which is still ongoing, by the way — writings which describe how I came back and was amongst you. I lived; I traveled; I had family; I knew you. I did not ascend and go off afar somewhere, where I could not be reached again except through intercessory prayer.

That was a great complexity thought up by the holy Child wanting to have some temporal power, desiring to have brothers and sisters believe that perhaps this one of the holy Child, known as the priest, priestess, was a bit more in touch with our Father than they could ever be. Therefore, whatever revelations were received by that priest, priestess, were of more value than what you received — a great untruth. But the belief was bought and the price was a bit dear, and now you have taken it back to the store and exchanged it for a better gift.

For truly, after the ascension which is recorded in your holy Scriptures, I came back and was amongst you for all of what you would see as your lifetime in that time, and there was much that was shared. Verily, I did not have just what you would see as three years with you. I came back to share the joy of the Father with you. I came to show you that the body is the manifestation of the Spirit, and that it is possible for one to lay down the body, to have it dead and buried, even consumed by the energy of fire, and it can be remanifest.

These are times when you will see that happening again. Already you feel the *presence* of ones who have laid down the body and you do not perhaps see the form, but you feel their presence. They speak to you and you speak with them. Sometimes you have thought you are just imagining it. But I would ask of you, what has occasioned the thought when you have thought of them? In other words, you may be doing something as mundane as the daily activities of washing dishes, taking the shower, driving the vehicle, and all of a sudden you will think upon this one. It is because they are knocking upon the door of your mind and heart and desiring acknowledgement.

They are very much with you, for, as you are all and they are all, they cannot go off somewhere where you would not be. As there has been a desire of your heart to know communication, communion, again with that one, that one desires it as much as you do. For I will share with you, to have a belief system where you would say that when the body is laid down, that is the end of the presence and the communication, is even more frustrating to the one who has laid down the body than it is for you.

For they want to be acknowledged. They are still alive — sometimes much to their surprise — and they want to be acknowledged. They want to be spoken to. They want to be included in your daily experience, and they call to you with great, great love and say, "Please do not shut me out." And you, because of a certain belief, respond, "That cannot be. I saw the body in the box. I saw the ashes of that body in the small cigar box. And I know that one is gone from me and I mourn the loss." And all the while that one is standing right next to you and saying, "See me. Hear me. Please!" Now, in the time of ascension you will be knowing yourself as the Light and the presence of Light, spirit, which is very much one with the others who are all around you. And you will walk through them, as they walk through you. Now, that is a thought to ponder.

You are upon the threshold of a time of ascension, a time of great joy, End Times, when there will be many messages and prophecies. Already you have them recorded in your holy Scriptures. Already you have the brothers and sisters most willing to share with you the prophecies. Already you have the masters who are coming to share with you messages of the end times, and all of them come because you have called them forth.

They do not come to trip you up. They do not come to bring dark forces upon this plane. For too long there has been belief in dark force. Do you know what dark force is? It is only the absence of the awareness, the *awareness*, of light. There is no force outside of you. There is no force that is going to overtake you and put you in darkness forever and ever. For indeed, you of your own making have experienced enough lifetimes of feeling in darkness. And where are you now? In other words, those lifetimes did not devastate you, did not put you in a place of the void where you were lost forever and ever. You are here right now with the hope, the possibility, the probability, the reality of unlimited Light and joy. That is where you stand right now.

So when ones speak to you of the possibility of evil forces, you may smile and say, "No, I've played that role. I know that role. Yes, I can relate to it." And perhaps there is a feeling of fear that will come up as ones would speak of the possibility of evil force, because you have already experienced it. Otherwise, it would be as the computer language that does not compute. But you have been there. You have experienced the times of darkness that you have brought upon yourself. You have experienced times of energy that seemed to be so powerful that the light would be almost extinguished.

You have brought forth in your experience times when you have used the energy of Spirit in such a forceful way that others felt a great motivation to lay down the body. As we have spoken, you cannot take from another one their form, their body. It is always a choice to release the body. But there can be seen to be great motivation to make the choice to release the body, and you have used the power of Spirit in such a way as to give motivation to brothers and sisters to lay down the body. You have been as the laser, the great laser beam that could split the crystal.

You have used the power of Spirit in most devastating ways, according to the judgment of ones on the other end of it. And you have been on the other end of it, so that you know the possibility of fear. So when ones would speak to you of the possibility of dark forces, of evil, there is a certain feeling that comes up to meet it, a feeling of relevancy, which says, "Yes, this is not beyond anything I could imagine. I can imagine this." But know you well that you have already completed that script. You are free now to choose for Love.

The end times are upon you. The prophecies, there will be many. There will be as many as there are brothers and sisters. There will be some seen as authorities because you have held them in a place of authority, although indeed they are your equal. But you have said, "Well, perhaps they know a bit more. Perhaps they are already ascended; therefore, they must know a bit more than I do."

As we have spoken, you have already ascended; otherwise you would not understand what I am speaking of. But you have yet the belief in process which says it will be in the future. So even the ascended masters are no more wise than you.

The ascended masters, if you will receive it, have their own perspective and they will give you their message from their perspective. For indeed what you call forth is still within the context of the belief system that you have agreed upon, so even as you would see ascended masters to be all wise and way above you, it is still part of the Adventure, the experience of the holy Child, and even the concept of ascended masters is a construct of the belief system.

Therefore, when you receive messages from ascended masters, from guides, from teachers, from loved ones even, allow yourself to sit in the place of the heart — and to breathe. For indeed some messages may come as a bolt of lightning out of the sky and may strike a place of fear with instant reaction because you know it well. It is most important to take the deep breath and then to return again unto the place of peace, the place of the heart, and to ask, "Is this truth for me?"

You as the holy Child, the collective brothers and sisters, are calling forth many messages. It is a time of information explosion. And this information is coming from many, many avenues and many, many channels because you have said, "I will know my Truth."

So ones will come and give you great opportunity to arrive at a place of clarity, a place of knowing. This is a time of sifting for you, of sifting the wheat from the chaff — not judging the chaff but just letting it go and taking to yourself the kernel of Truth. It is a time of harvest. It is a time when you are harvesting yourself. It is a time when you and many of the brothers and sisters will be willing to ascend and to be harvested, if you will use that analogy. Others will desire to stay within a certain belief system until they know completion with it.

After the harvest, will you still know experience? Of course. Will you know experience upon this plane, our Holy Mother, the Earth? Yes, if you so desire. Or you may say, "I want to try another expression." Then you will bring conscious focus of attention to that experience.

The end times: the end of an age, the end of the age of the belief that there could be separation from all that our Father is. Long enough have you nurtured your experience within the petri dish of separation. Now dawns the age, the time of ascension.

Graduation

Beloved and holy Child of our Heavenly Father, now dawns a time of great joy, a time of revelation and a time of graduation. You are one who has chosen to graduate, for you are ready to come unto the next level of understanding. You are embarking upon a time of upliftment, a time for which you have prepared yourself throughout all of your histories known as lifetimes.

You have known deep within your soul that this is the lifetime that you will bring together the remembrance of revelations and insights of all of the lifetimes of inspiration, and that you will bring them into an integration and an understanding in this point of time. You are birthing the remembrance of the Christ, and you are in process of moving in your understanding from what is known as the third dimension experience and expression into the fifth dimension. You experience from time to time the fourth as you allow yourself to go into meditation, into prayer, into that exalted state which allows you to connect with more than just what you see this personality and this expression to be.

There is a wave of energy being birthed upon this plane, the energy known as the fifth dimension, the dimension of Light and Love, where light will be most visibly expressed and love will be remembered as your true essence.

As you are willing to graduate, to leave behind a certain level of understanding which has served you well, and move into the next, there will be much that will change for you. You are called upon, as the graduate that you are, to live from the space of fifth dimension, the space of Light where you know yourself to be lighthearted and even light of form. You are now willing to come from the space of Love, looking upon all of the brothers and sisters with love in your heart, understanding that you have been in the space where they now see themselves to be; you can relate and respond with compassion.

Already you have experienced being the bridge of love between third and fifth dimensional expression as you have heard brothers and sisters speaking of their pain, their confusion, the issues which they felt themselves to be facing, and you have had empathy; you have understood. But you have also seen that their perception was temporary, born of identification with the temporal world, and that they were moving towards a grander vision, the holy vision.

And there have been times when you have been able to share your vision with one, to put the arm around that one, to share your insights, your experience, or the book which has come to hand —because you have called it forth — which is exactly the next steppingstone for that one in their unfoldment.

Now, as the graduate that you are, you have played with certain concepts. You have thought about, you have contemplated, you have read, you have discussed certain ideas, very basic questions which the soul brings up, such as, "Who am I?" At some point in every lifetime, every history, you and the brothers and sisters have asked, "Who am I?" And there have been the definitions which would vary according to the experience you were desiring to have in that lifetime.

There have been lifetimes when you saw yourself defined as the great warrior, the protector of the tribe. There have been lifetimes when you saw yourself defined as the priest, priestess, shaman, protector of the collective spiritual philosophy. There have been lifetimes when you answered the question of, "Who am I?" as, "I am the great teacher. I am the one who has researched all of the ancient scriptures, and I have studied the heavens, and I will share my insights with the brothers and sisters. That is who I am.

I am a master teacher." And yes, you have been and are.

But that did not fulfill the soul's yearning to know, to reconnect and to remember. And so in what you would see as the next recycling, the next experience of lifetime, there has been the question which has come again, "Who am I?" And you have kept asking over and over as you allowed yourself to come closer and closer to the remembrance of the whole Child that you are, the holy Child.

Many lifetimes you have felt lost, outcast and forgotten. Yet somehow, in a very distant memory which seems to be just beyond your grasp, you remember being part of the One, you remember Home, you remember the Family of the One. But you have felt yourself to be distant from your true Family; somehow you were sent here and then they lost your address.

And you have gone through your experiences. In this lifetime you have gone through your experiences of asking, "Why am I here?" There have been times known as the dark night of the soul when you have done much questioning, and you have said unto your Father, "I remember You. Deep within my heart, I remember You, but I do not feel You." And you have asked, "Why have You forgotten me? Why am I here?" And in time you have come to the revelation that you are the Father's Love upon this plane. You *are* the Love that you seek.

That is why you are here: to express Love in conscious awareness and realization in the fifth dimension. That is what you are graduating into. No longer governed by the belief in duality, you release the heavy chains of limited self-image. What you have hoped for, what you have prayed for, what you have remembered deep within the heart you will express and experience upon this plane.

You will come to realize — make real in your experience that which is already Real — the answer to your question of, "Why am I here?," a very basic, universal question, one which I asked of myself in my unfoldment and remembrance. I had heard the stories, the prophecies. I knew that I was to be messiah of my people. I did not know what that meant. They did not give me a job description.

And I asked, "Why me? Why am I here?" And as I communed with my Father, understanding myself to be His expression upon this plane, I received my answer, as you are now receiving your answer moment by moment, choice by choice.

As the graduate that you are, you have played with the concept of time. You have asked, "What is time? Why does time sometimes seem to stand still, and other times it goes too quickly? What is the purpose of time?" When you are awaiting something that is longed for, such as the realization of the vision which you hold deep within your heart, you have said, "I know that this can be and will be a reality upon this plane. Why is it not here yet, when I can see it? I can feel myself in alignment with the vision. Why is this still a bit far off?"

The purpose of time, as you have brought it forth, is to give yourself opportunity for choice: to hold a vision, to contemplate it, to see how it feels, to look at it one way and then another. It gives you opportunity, in your belief in process, to play with perspective and to experiment with choices *before* actualized manifestation. You, as the infinite being that you are, remember instant manifestation. You know that it is most possible to think a thought and to be right there, or to think a thought and have something manifest in front of you. That remembrance comes from the Truth of your being, for in Reality there is no time. But as you have agreed to experience the vibratory rate which has been a collective agreement upon this plane, you have agreed to a certain rate of process. And there have been times when you have fought against that and have known impatience.

There is an acceleration of energy upon this plane, and it seems like time itself is collapsing, for indeed it is. Time is of your own making. Time is your measurement of process, and because you are allowing yourself to accelerate into your Light expression, you are altering your perception of time.

In the days to come, which are right here, you will be experiencing acceleration of your own energy. Already you have been experimenting with how your energy feels. There have been times when you have felt most lighthearted, joyous, uplifted, enlightened, and your vibratory energy has accelerated in those moments. Ones looking upon you in that state of exhilaration, exultation, see a radiance, and they say to you, "You are glowing." And it is true.

You have also experienced times of deep depression, where your energy, as it would be measured, has been slowed down. You have allowed yourself to abide in that space for a time, and then by choice, outpictured in an infinite variety of reasons and means, you have brought it back up again, for it is the soul's nature to know joy, to express joy, to know the vibratory rate of joy.

Allow yourself a moment several times in your day to stop, to pause and to ask, "How does my energy feel? What is my vibratory rate at this moment? Am I feeling uplifted? Am I feeling in joy? Or am I feeling a bit heavy, weighted down by decisions or choices which 'must be' made?" Allow yourself to take stock. It is most important that you, the graduate, connect most consciously with the vibratory rate of your own Light energy, of what you are allowing to express through the very cells of the body.

Now, a word of caution. When you have taken stock in that moment, do not judge yourself. In other words, do not say, "Oh, I 'should' be feeling higher than this." You are doing a piece of research. You are not going to judge it. In fact, as we speak of judgment, how does that feel? Already you can feel the energy is being constricted. Do not judge, but take stock of it and then remember how it feels when you look upon the beauty of a sunset, when you look upon the beauty of a flower that is opening, when you look upon the love in the beloved pet's eyes, when you look upon the joy of a friend who loves you.

Remember the joy in a piece of humor, a story, an anecdote that allows the heart to be lightened in gentle — or exuberant —laughter. Remember the love light in the mate's eyes. Remember how it feels when a brother or a sister has a moment of insight and they feel whole for that moment. Remember the joy. And then take stock of where your vibratory rate is. You will have uplifted it.

Allow yourself to think upon times of beauty, times of love, times of understanding, times of insight, times of revelation, times of remembrance of the Love of the Father. There is a writing in your Scriptures, "Whatsoever things are true, whatsoever things are honorable, whatsoever things are just, whatsoever things are pure, whatsoever things are lovely, what-soever things are of good report, if there be any virtue and if there be any praise, think upon these things" that are uplifting. Allow yourself to dwell upon the beauty and the Love that you know so well.

For indeed, only the uplifted vibrations are going to go into the fifth dimension. For the fifth dimension is an accelerated experience of vibratory rate. Those who choose to abide in the rate that is now predomi-nant upon this plane will stay with that vibratory rate until they are desirous of experiencing the Light that they are. Verily, there is no judgment and there is no time. So it matters not in eternity, as you under-stand eternity to be, whether they choose in this life-time or billions of lifetimes later to experience the Light, the light body and the light expression. But they will not be within your realm of experience as you choose to go on to the next level of expression which has been named the fifth dimension, an accel-erated vibratory rate of Light.

Right now you are Light which is activating the form. There is a percentage of the Light that you are that is being directed consciously to activate the form, and you are now in process of going to the fifth dimension of awakened being, where you know you are the Light which pervades all of creation. The fifth dimension has also been called ascension, for indeed you will ascend into it. The ascension comes with the revelation and remembrance of the energy that activates the form. It comes from the place of the heart, of Love, and is a very dynamic expression of Love.

Allow yourself to get up at the break of dawn, and to feel the vibration of Mother Earth in the newness of the day, to behold with new eyes the beauty of creation. Now, if the body calls to you and you want to return unto bed, if that is your choice, there is no judgment with that either. Or if the employer decides that you must be with him at the crack of dawn, well, so be it. But allow yourself a moment to connect with the vibration of living as it is new in the morning.

Then allow yourself to connect with the vibration of living as it is in your eventide, and to see the beauty and the balance of each day, to know that you are the Lord who has brought forth that day. You are the one who is experiencing it. Verily, the day would not come forth to be experienced if you did not call it forth, and you may look upon it and call it good. Allow your heart to sing, to feel the upliftment as you behold the beauty which is all around you. You are the one who has put it there to remember the joy of creation. Creation is not something that was done a long time ago, afar off, all completed and finished. Creation is ongoing in every moment. You create every moment.

If you will receive it, you are in the process of creating fifth dimensional experience even now. It is not by accident that you hear so many of the brothers and sisters talking about a new Age, a new time upon this plane. You call forth the books, you call forth the teachers that talk about the ending of an age and the birthing of a new Age. There is a collective remembrance which is bringing forth a new dimension of expression of the Father's Love.

Now, are there truly different dimensions? Are there truly different levels?

Because there is a belief in duality/polarity upon this plane, there is also a belief in gradations and levels, and there is a belief in dimensions. The Truth of your being is that you are One already, that you are All, already. But you have agreed that you would bring a point of focus, a point of awareness, right here to experience how it feels to be very much that point of focus, totally immersed in the experience so that you know it intimately.

Never again will you choose to come and experience it this way, for you know it intimately. You are now choosing, because of the belief in progression and process, to say, "I will go into the next level of remembrance. I will graduate from a certain level of understanding to the place of claiming my master's degree."

Now, I will share with you what seems to be quite impossible from this point of belief: that when you get to what you now think of as fifth dimension, as you see it to be somewhere above you, you will not believe in levels. You will know Oneness of Light, unlimited, and you will know that Light is dynamic Love in expression, wherever you choose to see yourself expressing.

For yet a little while longer there is a belief in process which suggests and supports a belief in levels, in dimensions. And it serves you well, for it allows you to play with and to contemplate something beyond this point of focus. There is a remembrance deep within you as we speak of fifth dimension, as we speak of ascension, which does not yet have conscious relevancy in this plane, but there is a remembrance of how that feels and what it might be about.

There is also a belief yet held, because of the belief in levels, that there are others in other dimensions who are levels above you, ascended masters, who know it all. And that is true: I do.

And so do you.

When you come unto the fifth dimension of knowing that you are the Light and the Love of the Father, the one holy Child, you will not see levels above you. You will see Oneness. You will know Oneness. You will not put other brothers or sisters above you in your valuing — even the ones known as the ascended masters. But it serves you well now where you are in your belief to say that there are levels and to say that there are enlightened ones who are somehow quite far beyond what you think yourself to be, and that perhaps, "If I study hard enough, meditate well enough, perhaps I will get to the place of understanding at least what it might feel like to be an ascended master." Well, when you claim fifth dimension, you will be ascended and you will know your mastery. And what will that make you? An ascended master.

So when ones speak of different levels and say that the ascended masters are somehow above on another level, that serves your belief right now. It serves as the carrot in front of the horse. But I will share with you that that carrot will not always stay out in front of the horse, for you are the one who is calling it in and you will know yourself to be the carrot.

However, for now, it serves your belief to say that, "There is more of the whole that I will experience." It is the carrot out there that keeps you thinking, "Okay, I will understand more. I will allow myself to know more, to experience more." And that is well and good. You are willing to play with new concepts, new ideas which go beyond what is held within the accepted belief of this dimension. And as you play with new ideas, expanded concepts, they excite the mind, and the vibratory rate of you accelerates as you feel that excitement.

Now, that is also why, if you will receive it, you bring forth times of fear: you desire to know accelerated vibratory rate. You approach the desire rather obliquely perhaps, but you bring forth instances where you feel fear because you want to connect with the accelerated energy that you are. You love the amusement park rides known as the roller coasters, for there is a rising fear of, "What will happen to the body?" You desire to connect with your energy in its accelerated rate.

You have all experienced being in a place of fear where you thought, "Oh, my goodness. What is going to happen to me? I'd better do something quick." The experience in that moment was very much suggesting to you that you'd better get most busy and do something. But the underlying knowing was that, "I am my Father's Child, and I will come through this as I have come through all of the other adventures. But meantime, I really experience my energy."

However, you have also refined the experience of fear to a place where you feel it as an ongoing experience. It is no longer the momentary instantaneous example of fear as you would see with the wild animal which would come and threaten the form, where you had to deal with it immediately.

Now you bring forth the instances where there is an ongoing underlying fear which does not serve you well. It does not allow the acceleration of energy. The experience of the subtle fear, all pervasive, comes to the surface from time to time, and, as you are vigilant, you can make choice and you can release it. Breathe, beloved one. Relax in the Father's Love.

As the graduate that you are, you have come to a place of contemplating — perhaps not claimed yet, but contemplating — the answer to, "Who am I?" You have caught a glimpse that makes you want to know and experience more. And you have caught a glimpse, an understanding of, "Why am I here?" And you have caught a glimpse and an understanding of the purpose of time and why time is collapsing as you allow your own energy to accelerate. Time seems to go fast when you are having fun because you are more into your true Self. When you are in your joy, you are allowing yourself to experience an acceleration of your energy. Other times when you are feeling a bit down about something, time seems slow. The need for time will dissolve at the point of ascension, at the point of knowing, "I am one." Then you will decree where you want to go as the Light being that you are, free to go. You will find yourself wherever you choose to be instantaneously.

You are at a choice point — you as a seeming individual, and you collectively as all of the brothers and sisters. It is a choice point, a time of choice. Those who do not choose to move on to the fifth dimension will go on experiencing and expressing; they will not go into a great void and be lost forever. The Light cannot be lost forever.

They will be experiencing and expressing, as they so choose, on this planet, but not as you will know this planet, our holy Mother, the Earth, to be. They will still be expressing and experiencing on what they will equate to be a planet known as Earth, Terra. But it will not be Terra, Mother Earth, as you know it to be. In other words, what you feel yourself to be experiencing right now is your agreement of reality. And even now, in what you see as the space that you occupy, there are other societies and cultures existing —dimensions you will call them — that are very much real to the beings who have chosen to experience that reality.

The wave of consciousness which is sweeping across the face of our holy Mother, the Earth, is a wave which is ushering in your reality, the fifth dimension. Others will be making their choices. Some will continue to abide in conflict, in greed, in jealousy, in fear, in hatred, in violence because they have not finished with the chocolate pudding.

Others of the brothers and sisters will participate in the reality of the fifth dimension without labeling it as such. Indeed, there are many that you would term innocent, who do not study the metaphysics, who are very much in knowing their oneness with the Life that they are. They are very much in the heart of extending care and support and love unto others, and they do not trouble themselves in what they see as this lifetime to understand the why's and wherefore's of philosophy. They just live it.

You are living your graduation. Every moment in every day is an opportunity for graduation as you leave behind the limited understanding, the limited image of who you have thought yourself to be, and you claim your remembrance of Who you are. "Who am I? I am the Christ." "Why am I here? To experience and express the Christ, to bring it into total manifestation, known as the Light of Heaven, upon this plane." Your graduation foretells the holiness of the days to come.

Teachers of God

Beloved one, in the time of miracles dawning now upon your plane many of you will be finding new choices coming up for you —options, alternatives, ideas. And you will sit with them and you will find yourself getting excited about one of them, or maybe several, and then the voice of the world may click in and say, "But you are already so busy; how can you fit that into your schedule? You have responsibilities here; how can you think of...?" You know the questions of the world all too well.

However, you are the one who has made the schedule, you are the one who perceives a limitation, and if you desire something, know that it holds great revelation for you. Return to the place of the heart, breathing quietly and effortlessly, sitting in silence. Abide with the desire, idea, option, and ask of it to reveal its inner meaning. Sit with the desire and see where you would like to be, what you would like to do. And if it brings joy to the heart, know that it is your right path. Desires are your teachers — as you are a teacher.

All of you are teachers. All of you are servants one unto another. Your brothers and sisters watch you even though you may not be aware of their observance. Each one watches to see how you view the world and, as you have new insights, the inner wisdom that you allow to come forth is shared with your brothers and sisters. For as you find the courage to speak your Truth and to say, "Yes, I find joy in my heart," you allow others to entertain the idea that perhaps there is joy in their heart as well. Perhaps, if they look for it, they will find it, and it is not something that has passed them by.

Each of you is a teacher. You teach what you live. Never think that what you do has small meaning, for everywhere you go, your presence is felt. Everyone that your energy touches, feels it. Every blade of grass, every flower, every tree feels your energy, and if you are in a depression, as it is called, they will know the frequency. If you are in a place of happiness, they will resonate.

You are very much in interaction with each other, and with all of creation. You do not live your life alone. The body may speak unto you that there is separateness. The body may suggest that there is boundary where one individual ends and another begins. And yet, the energy that you are is not, cannot be, contained within the body. As we have spoken many times, it is the energy of you that activates the body.

All of you are teachers. Teach the Love of our Heavenly Father. This was my message unto the disciples. This is my message unto you in this day. *You* are my disciples as you do the work of our Father. And it is not a work of effort. It is a work of joy. You are my disciples as you allow yourself to express the very dynamic Love that you are.

Teach the Love of God. Teach Who you are. Speak words of encouragement. Speak words of joy. Allow others to tell their story, yes, for it is necessary for them to have clarity about what they are feeling. But after a certain clarity has been reached, encourage them to see the broader vision. Allow them to see what you have seen: the Love that activates every living thing. Share with them a (w)holier perspective — and it need not be expressed in words that you would see as coming from your holy Scriptures. You do not need to stand upon the soapbox and to thump, I believe the word is, your holy Scriptures.

Look for the beauty in the world. Search for it, for it is there. Focus upon beauty, live in the beauty of each moment, teach beauty. There is no grander task than to remember the Love that has brought forth beauty.

Be the teacher of Love.

Be the teacher of God.

As you read these words, I touch you gently. I call forth the joy that abides deep within you. I encourage you to remember the time before time when you played in the meadow of your Father's Kingdom, secure in His Love. He has never left you, nor you Him. Claim now your birthright as His only begotten Child, the Christ, and ascend unto Me.

So be it.

Oakbridge University Press

Publishers of metaphysical books and materials

The books that we publish reflect our desire to support and encourage the emerging consciousness of Light and Love, and to assist the awakening of all humanity in Oneness.

Jeshua: The Personal Christ, Volume I

Channeled information from Jeshua ben Joseph — Jesus. We hear about reincarnation, channeling, love, earth changes, ego, the divine feminine, ascension and more. We are reminded of the simplicity and love of Jesus' message to us. Contains a beautiful meditation.

$12.95 Tradepaper   150 pages

Jesus Speaks: Don't Look for Me in a Tortilla Chip, Volume III

In this volume, Jeshua/Jesus speaks to you about the writings of the Bible more fully. Passages such as the Ten Commandments, The Sermon on the Mount, The Beatitudes take on new and expanded meaning. In a very personal way Jesus describes His baptism and temptations, choosing His disciples and beginning His ministry. "Beloved one, do not seek me in the outer; seek me where I may be found — in your heart."

Mother Mary talks about Holy Communion.

$12.95 Tradepaper   200 pages

Jesus and Mastership: The Gospel According to Jesus of Nazareth

Jesus tell His story in His own words. Dictated through the Rev. James C. Morgan, this is the day to day account of Jesus' life from age 18, when He went to India to study, through the crucifixion and resurrection. He tells of choosing His disciples, His relationship with Miriam, His ministry and why He taught what He did.

$14.95 Tradepaper   390 pages indexed

Yes, I would like to order the following books:

Please send (quantity)

___ Jeshua: The Personal Christ I $12.95

___ Jeshua: The Personal Christ II $12.95

___ Jeshua: Don't Look for Me in a Tortilla Chip
      Vol. III $12.95

___ Jesus and Mastership $14.95

Please include postage of $3.50, plus $1.00 for
each additional book.

Enclosed is $_____

Name _____

Address _____

City _____ State ___ Zip ____

Telephone _____

Visa/Mastercard information:

Account # _____

Expiration Date _____

Signature _____

Oakbridge University Press
4007 Harbor Ridge Rd NE
Tacoma, WA 98422
(253) 952-3285
www.oakbridge.org